*Green Series*

# GREENING YOUR
# COTTAGE
# OR VACATION
# PROPERTY
## Reduce Your Recreational Footprint

Joan Bartley & Tracy Bartley

**Self-Counsel Press**
*(a division of)*
International Self-Counsel Press Ltd.
USA     Canada

Self-Counsel Press acknowledges the financial support of the Government of Canada through the Canada Book Fund (CBF) for our publishing activities.

Printed in Canada.

First edition: 2017

**Library and Archives Canada Cataloguing in Publication**

Bartley, Joan, author
    Greening your cottage or vacation property : reduce your recreational footprint / Joan Bartley & Tracy Bartley.

(Green series)
(Self-counsel reference)
Includes bibliographical references and index.
Issued in print and electronic formats.
ISBN 978-1-77040-290-4 (softcover).—ISBN 978-1-77040-482-3 (EPUB).—
ISBN 978-1-77040-483-0 (Kindle)

    1. Sustainable living. 2. Vacation homes. I. Bartley, Tracy, author II. Title. III. Series: Self-counsel reference series IV. Series: Self-Counsel green series

| GE196.B37 2017 | 640.28'6 | C2017-902366-7 |
| | | C2017-902367-5 |

**Self-Counsel Press**
*(a division of)*
International Self-Counsel Press Ltd.

| Bellingham, WA | North Vancouver, BC |
| USA | Canada |

# Contents

# Notice to Readers

Laws are constantly changing. Every effort is made to keep this publication as current as possible. However, the author, the publisher, and the vendor of this book make no representations or warranties regarding the outcome or the use to which the information in this book is put and are not assuming any liability for any claims, losses, or damages arising out of the use of this book. The reader should not rely on the author or the publisher of this book for any professional advice. Please be sure that you have the most recent edition.

# Dedication

We dedicate this book to Ken Bartley — husband, dad, grandpa — whose building and construction knowledge and love of the land is forever with us at our island cottage.

# Introduction

*You said you need the tree for its pulp,*
*You'd take but a few, you're aware*
*Of the home of the deer, the wolf, the fox,*
*Yet so much of their land now stands bare ...*
*If the beauty around us is to live through this day*
*We'd better start watching — and care.*

— David Bouchard, Roy Henry Vickers

A cottage, or vacation property, has as many reasons for being as there are properties and cottagers. However, one thing we can all relate to is the relationship between lifestyle choices at the cottage, and our shared environment. Greening one's cottage, inside and out, is an opportunity to make an environmentally conscious commitment to learn about and work towards a sustainable environment for our children, grandchildren, and beyond.

Our cottage vision, (yes, we created a vision statement for our cottage and we'll cover how you can too, in Chapter 1), expresses our greening journey towards an environmentally sustainable lifestyle. Yours can be tailored to your cottage, property, and personality.

Our cottage vacation property is on land belonging to the Coast Salish people. Today, constant reminders of that past come to mind as we cohabitate with the fauna and flora of this Canadian, west coast vacation property. The setting is quiet. Our little cottage and vacation property is on an island, hidden within a new-growth forest of giant Douglas Fir, cedar, and grand fir. (This land has been victimized by clear cutting.) The relentless crashing of the ocean's waves against the sandstone beaches contributes to the naturally peaceful setting.

Grandchildren explore the forest, draw and paint their curiosities, organize the recycling, and plan for their tomorrows. This is nature's classroom where three generations of family members learn, work, and play.

At our family cottage, living in harmony with nature is the very essence of our lifestyle choice. It was clear right from the outset that this rural property was begging for an eco-conscious stewardship, and that's what we aim to give it.

The cottage was already 15 years old when we made our decision to purchase. It had been mindfully built and was of sound construction. Many salvaged materials and fixtures such as energy-efficient double-glazed windows, doors, and kitchen cabinetry were sourced from previous dwellings. The appliances were all as old as the cottage, yet in good working order. Outbuildings, such as a woodshed, garden/storage shed, and water system shed were in an unfinished state. Over the years the grounds had acquired quite a bit of Scotch broom (a noxious weed), and fallen branches and trees, creating a fire hazard. The potential to restore this property was obvious, yet there was work to be done.

Immediately we began recycling, repurposing, and reusing; we had begun our greening process. However, there was much to learn about greening, and a need to prioritize in order to determine a plan of action: a greening action plan. Our goal was to reduce our environmental footprint and attain a sustainable lifestyle; that is, we wanted to restore and conserve our natural resources, to invest in eco-friendly upgrades, and ultimately to attain a long-term environmental balance inside and outside our cottage.

# 1. Purpose of This Book

The purpose of this book is to show cottagers, across the generations and a wide variety of locations and builds, that they can make a difference to the wellness of the environment. Based on one family's journey at one cottage, this book illustrates a greening process which is planned, practical, flexible, and adaptable.

The chapters take you through a vision-constructing process, setting out with the end in mind, and closing with substantive greening actions and reflections.

Throughout the book, environmentally conscious projects and actions are described in everyday terms complemented with personal stories and experiences. In some instances, environmental concerns, particularly those resulting from years of consumerism and perceived convenience, are discussed as they pertain to various aspects of greening at the cottage, and as a reminder that human actions have caused great havoc to the environment. Yet we wish to bring a message of hope; that greening your cottage, inside and out, can make a positive difference towards environmental sustainability.

Greening strategies, eco-friendly tips, and reflective practices are provided, and readers are given the challenge to create a Cottage Greening Action Plan to put into place at their own cottages or vacation properties.

A list of websites and books for further reading, including children's literature, is shared on the download kit included with this book.

# I
# Getting Started: Crafting Your Vision Statement

*... cleaner energy and a healthier Earth are within our reach as long as we remain attentive and committed to a vision of a world in which our perceived needs are not always placed first.*

— Lori Ryker

Getting started at greening your cottage is a vision-constructing process, setting out with an end in mind: a greening goal. Thus, the process starts with goal-setting: What do you expect to accomplish as a result of your greening commitment?

Your goal is the foundation upon which your vision will be crafted, and, your vision (put into a statement) puts into context your goal. A vision describes a broader picture of values, aspirations, and greening actions. Your cottage greening vision statement will express how your greening goal will ultimately look, sound, and feel.

# 1. Defining Greening and Sustainability

It is important to define "greening" and "sustainability" before we move on. Greening encompasses the conscious practices taken to attain an environmentally sustainable lifestyle. Greening your cottage will become influential to your transitioning lifestyle. You will notice that your greening practices or habits will evolve and grow, becoming a natural way of living. Over time, your lifestyle will become one which nurtures sustainability.

Sustainability is the ultimate goal of greening where everyone at the cottage, or associated with the cottage, works toward a sustainable lifestyle. A sustainable lifestyle will enable nature to re-establish her original role of checks and balances to restore and conserve a healthy self-sustaining environment.

Greening and sustainability, two interrelated concepts, are integral to what we are discussing in this book and what you are attempting to do. These two concepts will take on a deeper meaning as you work through your vision-constructing process. With conscious and persistent greening, sustainability can become a reality.

# 2. Setting Your Greening Goal

Setting your greening goal needs to be a collaborative effort in order to engage all family members, partners, or co-owners: you and your fellow cottagers. What do you we want your greening goal to be? Ask yourself and your fellow cottagers: What do we expect to accomplish as a result of our collective greening commitment?

As the title of this book suggests, a sustainable lifestyle is the ultimate greening goal. This is lofty; indeed, it is within reach. Your goal may seem far off, or even unattainable at first. Greening goals are based upon individuals' knowledge and understanding of a variety of environmental concepts, issues, strategies, actions, and practices. Think about all of these when considering your possible cottage lifestyle goal. Your goal may be focused on: energy efficiency, renewable resources, greenhouse gases (GHGs), zero waste, nurturing nature, or, whatever you and your fellow cottagers feel will be fitting to your values and greening commitment.

Begin the conversation, with yourself if you're a solo cottager, or with family members or partners, if you have co-owners or partners in the property. What do you expect to accomplish as a result of our greening at the cottage, inside and out?

The following greening actions may be helpful conversation starters as you explore and consider a possible goal or goals for your cottage greening journey:

- Restoring and conserving nature.

- Conserving natural resources.

- Investing in eco-friendly upgrades.

- Minimizing stuff.

- Renovating, or building a cottage, with reclaimed and salvaged materials.

- Retrofitting with renewable materials and resources.

- Reducing the carbon footprint: greenhouse gases.

- Zero waste management.

- Becoming energy efficient.

- Building a sustainable cottage.

Rest assured, whatever your greening goal (and subsequent greening vision), environmental benefits will be realized at the cottage, and beyond. Getting started at greening your cottage has the potential for multiple positive effects upon your health; the health of your family; the health and well-being of your community; and in the long term, the health of the environment.

# 3. Exploring and Visioning: What Lifestyle and Environmental Values Define Your Ultimate Cottage Experience?

This is a question to reflect upon in order to set a context for one's greening goal: What is your ultimate greening vision? Explore your values and desired lifestyle aspirations, particularly in view of working towards an environmentally sustainable lifestyle. How will your vision describe how your greening goal at the cottage looks, sounds, and feels? It is important to understand that a vision-constructing process can be challenging, and messy!

Though sustainability is the ultimate result of greening, it may appear too idealistic a focus for your greening vision, at least for the time being. A greening vision will vary from cottager to cottager and locale to locale, and take on a very personal and introspective approach towards a desired cottage lifestyle, and beyond.

There are as many responses to this as there are cottages and cottagers. A few familiar replies are: "This is where I get away from it all to relax and to refresh." "It is our haven away from the city." "I yearn to get back to nature." "This is our quality family time."

It seemed that all of the above, and more, was important to our family's cottaging ideals. Fortunately for our family, we rented several cottages within our island community before making the decision to become cottage owners. As renters, we found ourselves surrounded by the flora and fauna of the west coast rainforest; and we became armored with our closeness to nature. At the same time, we learned about and valued the environmentally conscious culture of the community.

Our first rental experience impacted our eventual greening plan immensely. The owner's message to us read: "You are responsible for the removal of your garbage upon your departure." With a baby in our family, there was definitely garbage. This meant learning about the community's already progressive recycling program, composting our biodegradable waste, and/or packing up and removing our refuse upon our departure. We did all three; and we learned that most of our non-recyclable and non-compostable refuse was composed of packaging, and disposable baby diapers!

Immersed in nature, and joining a community where greening was more the norm than the exception, became an imminent calling to green our cottage inside and out. Our cottage already possessed integrity, sustainability wise. It was consciously constructed with locally sourced cedar products, salvaged and reclaimed cabinetry and doors, and energy-efficient, double glazed windows. Furthermore, it was situated on a beautiful, forested rural property! A cottage surrounded by nature, three generations of family members to share the responsibility, and a collective will and understanding that there would be a lot to learn and do: We were ready to green our cottage.

Because nature was so influential to the joy of our cottage life, greening the cottage extended beyond the walls of the cottage. There was a natural interconnectedness between the cottage and the property. And, based upon the desire to build upon what we already saw as valuable greening attributes at our cottage, we saw a sustainable environmental goal as being inherent. With reflection, excited anticipation, and exploration, a vision began to emerge into words.

Figure 1: A glimpse at our cottage life

Our vision involved:

- Escaping from the city.

- Relaxing and rejuvenating.

- Restoring and conserving nature.

- Spending quality time together.

- Quiet.

- Living in harmony with nature.

- Committing to a greening lifestyle.

- Embracing a minimalist lifestyle.

- Reflecting.

- Renovating with reclaimed and renewable resources and materials.

- Practicing zero waste.

Your greening vision may involve a single value, or several values encompassing the ideal cottage lifestyle for you.

If you are starting with a blank slate or are in the planning stages of building a new cottage, it makes sense that your vision includes sustainable building strategies. At the very least, consider reclaimed building materials and incorporate the infrastructure for renewable clean energy sources, such as geothermal heating and cooling, solar energy, or rain water catchment.

If you are starting with an established property, your vision can be based on the greening strategies and practices you already have in place, along with those you would like to see realized, as time and finances afford. Your Taking Stock checklist, (Checklist 1 discussed in Chapter 2), will help you determine a realistic starting point.

How do you want your cottage experience or lifestyle to look, sound, and feel? Explore this as you brainstorm several possible greening visions. Think big. A greening vision is about looking to the future.

It appears many cottagers, once exploring and engaging in a vision-constructing process, soon feel the urge to get to work. In fact, many see this as a prime time to explore a greening action which they have read or heard about. Exploration helps to form and inform your greening vision, and to build confidence: You can do this!

# 4. Get to Work Straightaway: What Can You Do Now?

The excitement, anticipation, and exploration is an opportunity to get to work, even before the vision itself is fully crafted. Spend time with your family, and other cottagers, talking about your dreams, aspirations, or needs. Search the Internet, pick up some cottage magazines at your bookstore, or visit your local library for current books on greening. Do not overlook the children's section at the library; it is teeming with informative and practical books to engage younger cottagers too. (See the download kit included with this book for many resources you may wish to explore.)

Gain insights from your cottage neighbors. What community greening actions are happening at their cottages and in the community, particularly with respect to waste management? Think about how you can improve your own greening habits, or how you can fit into the current eco-friendly culture of your cottage neighborhood. A place for you to take immediate action may appear as you re-examine your recycling habits. Think about how you can:

- Reuse.

- Repair.

- Repurpose.

- Multipurpose.

Of course, with practicing to reduce recyclables comes other realizations. Perhaps your shopping habits will take on a noticeable change. Purchases with reduced packaging, or better still, no packaging at all, may become your choices. When quality items, such as stainless steel and wooden garden tools are purchased, they will long outlive cheaper plastic tools that you may be tempted to buy. A minimalist cottage lifestyle may be something worth exploring, too.

Start to reduce your trash. Reducing the trash that ends up in our overused landfill sites also reduces the harmful toxins and greenhouse gases polluting our air and contaminating our water supplies. Think about how your actions to reduce recyclables, or to make environmentally conscious shopping choices, will influence the crafting of your cottage greening vision. (There is more in Chapter 2 about common greening practices.)

# 5. Crafting Your Cottage Greening Vision Statement

Once you've decided on your greening goal at your cottage or vacation property — you have reflected upon your lifestyle and environmental values, you have started to reduce your recyclables (or other greening actions), and you have set your sights on your desired cottage lifestyle or experience — you can begin working on your Cottage Greening Vision Statement.

Set out with the end in mind, which means understand and reflect upon your greening goal, the foundational target for your greening vision.

Your vision will put meaning and context to your goal. Once again ask yourself: How will my vision describe how my greening goal at the cottage looks, sounds, and feels?

Collectively ponder and reflect on your ideal cottage lifestyle and your developing vision. Put your greening vision into words, and be prepared to revisit and to revise until everyone comes to an agreeable understanding.

After this often exhausting process, it is well worth sharing your vision. Allow the artist at your cottage, if you have one, to creatively represent your vision, or frame and hang it in your cottage to celebrate your collective efforts and for ongoing reference and reflection.

Or maybe you are more interested in going digital and would rather upload your greening vision to a shared file on a cloud, or create your own cottage greening website or blog.

Tips for crafting your own greening vision:

- Revisit and rethink your greening goal: What is this all about?

- Brainstorm: How will our greening lifestyle look, sound, and feel at our cottage?

- Mind map or explore possible vision statements.

- Reflect and revise.

- Come to consensus.

- Represent, or put into words, your Cottage Greening Vision.

Your Cottage Greening Vision Statement needs to be valued by all who contributed to its development, and by all who frequent your cottage. It is everyone's responsibility to share the commitment which will be involved in the work and the learning along your greening journey.

## Example 1
# A Cottage Greening Vision Statement

**A gift of nature and place; a place of stewardship, sustainability, and solitude.**
Creating a lifestyle of curiosity, respect, creativity, and stewardship,
for our children, grandchildren, great-grandchildren ...
Living a "green" environmentally friendly ethos is envisioned as we connect
with nature, deepen our understandings, nurture our spirits,
and refurbish our little island cottage in its big forest.

Keep in mind that collectively, every Cottage Greening Vision has the potential to count towards a sustainable lifestyle, and a healthier environment! Your next steps in the process of planning for and taking action to green your cottage, inside and out, will involve taking stock. Now that you know what your goals and your vision are, an inventory of the building construction and materials, the finishing features and installations, and your current cottage greening habits will be examined in the following chapter so you can act upon them later.

# 2
# Taking Stock Inside and Out

*If it can't be reduced, reused, repaired, rebuilt, refurbished, refinished, resold, recycled, or composted, then it should be restricted, redesigned or removed from production.*

— Pete Seeger

Now that you've figured out your goal(s) and decided on a vision, your next steps to greening the cottage inside and out are about identifying what eco-friendly sources and resources, energy-efficient attributes, and sustainable lifestyle habits are currently in place at the cottage. Thus, you will get an idea of how green things already are at the cottage, and therefore what sort of projects could be imminent.

> There were three key factors which influenced our decision to purchase a 15-year-old island cottage on five acres of west coast rainforest: the obvious small footprint of the cottage, the sufficient supply of potable well-water, and, the majestic forest of fir and cedar. The cottage was constructed from local cedar, and reclaimed and salvaged materials and fixtures. The salvaged windows, for example, were expansive

double glazed units offering a high insulation factor, allowing for an abundance of natural lighting, and serving to connect our living space to the forest; the natural habitat of deer, raccoons, ravens, frogs, and numerous creatures too small to observe. A large wraparound deck integrated the forest into our everyday living space. The kitchen cabinetry and bathroom fixtures were reclaimed and salvaged units, and in keeping with the concept of reclaiming and reusing materials, along with the cottage purchase, we inherited a 15-year-old electric range and refrigerator, both in good working order. Clearly, a landfill site (which in reality does not exist on our island) was potentially spared of these building materials and appliances, at least for the time being. With such environmentally conscious features in place, we realized that we had a responsibility to continue along the path of sustainability which our newly purchased cottage had launched for us. Greening appeared to be an inevitable commitment.

Our exercise in taking stock had its beginning with the cottage inspection report that we received from an inspector hired at the time of our placing an offer on the property. This report offered some guidance in determining the quality of the construction and the nature of the materials. Much reading and conferring also took place as we anticipated that we were about to embark upon a greening journey, and that we had much to learn. We took a serious look at our current greening habits, and where we needed to deepen our knowledge and understanding of greening. A greening commitment meant there was going to be a lot of work and learning ahead.

# 1. Taking Stock

Taking stock is an exercise similar to taking an inventory. This exercise allows you to pay attention to what is currently green at your cottage, and what your current greening practices look like. The purpose of taking stock is to:

- Identify the green attributes that your cottage already possesses.

- Assess the quality of the greening habits you are currently practicing at the cottage.

- Determine the gaps and needs which you will plan to take action upon: What's next, or what needs to change?

Taking stock will assist in assessing the greening integrity of the cottage and of the cottagers, specifically: renewable resources, energy-efficient features, carbon footprint, and the cottagers' commitment to greening. Considering your greening vision, ponder these two questions:

- What eco-friendly attributes are now in place at the cottage?

- What greening habits are happening right now?

Taking stock will shed light upon these two questions, and make way for what will need to improve or change.

If you feel that you need additional help in deciding what should change, do not hesitate to ask advice from a tradesperson, contractor, or an informed friend. This is particularly important if your cottage is of older construction. The codes and standards for electrical wiring, plumbing, heating, and septic systems change over the years not only to improve safety factors, but also to meet higher energy efficiency and environmental standards. Ways you can determine an approximate installation date of a septic system, for example, include: checking the system permit or installation certificate (if available); looking for a manufacturer's date on the pump housing, switch, or tank lid; or asking a realtor or neighbor in the area who may have an idea of when the system was installed. Knowing the approximate age of the infrastructure of the cottage and its systems, and gathering some information on what new eco-friendly products are currently available will assist you in determining and prioritizing what needs to change.

## 1.1 Categories for taking stock

Categories, or areas to focus the taking stock exercise, can differ from locale to locale. For example, the energy source at a cottage development or community may differ considerably from that of an off-grid cottage. If the cottage is connected to a community water supply and sanitation system, this too will differ from a locale where wells and septic systems are the norm. Categories may also vary somewhat if you have just purchased a cottage, or if you have had the cottage over a number of years. If an inspection report was completed at the time of purchase, this too may suggest categories to consider during your exercise of taking stock. Generally speaking, categories, or broad areas which can guide the taking stock exercise include, though are not limited to:

- **Cottage construction:** foundation, frame, exterior finishing, roofing, windows.

- **Infrastructure:** insulation, energy source (electrical or other), plumbing, heating and cooling.

- **Interior features:** finishing, large appliances, furnishings, kitchenware.

- **Water and sewage:** community, or well and septic systems.

- **Grounds:** landscaping, outbuildings, other.

- **Current greening practices at the cottage:** How does greening at the cottage currently look?

Your first steps may be basic. Or, you may want to construct a detailed checklist similar to Checklist 1 (a blank copy has been included on the download kit). Whether the list of categories is short or long, this inventory-like exercise allows you to assess through an environmental lens, what needs to change in order to move toward an environmentally sustainable lifestyle.

Taking stock will immediately shed light upon what you will need to repair, upgrade, refurbish, or retrofit, and, what greening habits you will need to improve upon to live your cottage greening vision.

## 1.2 Taking stock checklist

Checklist 1 may assist you in taking stock of what greening attributes currently look like at your cottage, inside and out. Note that a simple rating scale, or assessment, has been included to create a baseline from which to move forward. With the information gathered through taking stock, you will be able to reflect on and think about the overall state, or quality, of "greenness." How green are you right now?

This checklist is an example only. It may serve as guidance in determining your next steps towards your eco-friendly sustainable vision.

Think of it as a picture of your current understanding of the greenness of your property and know that everything will evolve as you learn more.

When you go through your checklist:

- Reflect upon your greening vision.

- Create or adapt a checklist to your liking, noting the building construction, infrastructure, materials, fixtures, and daily greening practices.

# Checklist I
# Taking Stock

| VISION:<br><br>... Living a "green" environmentally friendly ethos is envisioned as we connect with nature, deepen our understandings, nurture our spirits, and refurbish our little island cottage in its big forest. | *What eco-friendly attributes are in place now?* | *What needs to change?*<br>i.e. repair, replace, retrofit, refurbish, install, apply, etc. | *Why greening?*<br>• Reduce waste<br>• Energy efficient features<br>• Renewable resources<br>• Eco-friendly materials<br>• Carbon footprint/GHG<br>• Nurture nature |
|---|---|---|---|
| **Taking Stock** | **Observation Notes** | **To Do** | **To Research** |
| **Cottage construction and finishing**<br>• foundation<br>• frame<br>• exterior<br>• roof<br>• windows | • 8 x 8 posts; concrete footings<br>• Wood frame<br>• Cedar inside and out<br>• Cedar shakes<br>• Double glazed windows (reclaimed)<br>• Screened windows: kitchen, bedroom, loft<br>• Treated wraparound wood deck | • Consult engineer re: upgrade supporting beams under deck and back of cottage<br>• Screens for bathroom, kids' sleep area<br>• Install metal rain gutters; 3" downspout<br>• Replace weather stripping | • Metal roofing: compare with asphalt shingles and cedar shakes<br>• Treated wood—environmental effect? |
| **Infrastructure**<br>• insulation<br>• energy source<br>• plumbing<br>• heating and cooling | • Hydro electric energy<br>• Electric baseboard heaters<br>• Wood stove (auxiliary heat)<br>• Ceiling fan | • Check electrical panel/wiring for Amp upgrade<br>• Repair/replace leaking taps | • Insulation: What is the R-value?<br>• Research wood heating<br>• 200 A; upgrade to 400 A |
| **Interior**<br>• finishing<br>• appliances | • Painted gyproc on interior walls<br>• Cedar ceiling and baseboards | • Replace toilet with dual flush 4.8 l. | |

| | | | |
|---|---|---|---|
| • furnishings & kitchenware | • Clay tile flooring throughout<br>• Reclaimed/salvaged cabinetry<br>• Shower<br>• Toilet (8l)<br>• Electric stove, refrigerator (1994) | • Check/monitor working order of stove and fridge.<br>• Wood table from Ikea | |
| **Water & Sewage**<br>• community<br>• well<br>• septic systems | • Septic tank and field<br>• Well water tested and potable! | • Have septic tank cleaned and inspected | |
| **Grounds**<br>• landscaping<br>• outbuildings<br>• other: | • Five acres new growth Douglas fir and cedar forest<br>• Scotch broom infestation<br>• Windfall debris, hazardous trees<br>• Open sunny space for<br>• dig in compost piles<br>• Small meadow and salal shrubbery | • Consult arborist for forest restoration- learn the names of the trees!<br>• Hire help to pull broom!<br>• Outbuildings: repair and finish garden shed & pump house | • Hire helper to buck windfall and hazardous trees around cottage. |
| **Greening Habits**<br>• recycling<br>• composting<br>• renewable resources<br>• reclaiming resources<br>• conserving nature<br>• conserving energy | • Recycle regularly<br>• Set up compost piles | • Set up recycling system in garden shed<br>• Furnish, stock with family cast-offs<br>• Go thrifting!<br>• Install outdoor clothesline to dry laundry outdoors | • Attend local Trust meetings |
| **Other:** | | | |

| ASSESSMENT How "green" are we? | Assess the overall quality of "green" using this simple rating scale, or one of your choice. |
|---|---|
| Energy efficient | Never ⇒ ⇒ ⇒ ⇒ ⇒ ⇒ ⇒ Sometimes⇒ ⇒ ⇒ ⇒ ⇒ ⇒ ⇒ Usually⇒ ⇒ ⇒ ⇒ ⇒ ⇒ ⇒ Consistently |
| Renewable resources | Never ⇒ ⇒ ⇒ ⇒ ⇒ ⇒ ⇒ Sometimes⇒ ⇒ ⇒ ⇒ ⇒ ⇒ Usually⇒ ⇒ ⇒ ⇒ ⇒ ⇒ ⇒ Consistently |
| Green House Gases | Never ⇒ ⇒ ⇒ ⇒ ⇒ ⇒ ⇒ Sometimes⇒ ⇒ ⇒ ⇒ ⇒ ⇒ ⇒ Usually⇒ ⇒ ⇒ ⇒ ⇒ ⇒ ⇒ Consistently |
| Greening habits | Never ⇒ ⇒ ⇒ ⇒ ⇒ ⇒ ⇒ Sometimes⇒ ⇒ ⇒ ⇒ ⇒ ⇒ Usually⇒ ⇒ ⇒ ⇒ ⇒ ⇒ ⇒ Consistently |
| **Reflections** | Our cottage has been constructed with a minimal footprint. It will be important that we work at maintaining and sustaining the integrity of the cottage; and at restoring and managing the forested property. There is much to learn: renewable resources; energy efficient upgrades; reducing GHGs; and more. <br><br> Just by looking at our current greening practices, there are learning opportunities and actions which we can immediately start from our *To Do* List. This is exciting. This is an opportunity to improve upon and to change our greening lifestyle right now. Let's get to reducing GHGs. What will this look like in one, or five years? Everyone, across our intergenerational family can do this! |

- Determine a simple rating scale, i.e., Met/Not Met; No Evidence/ Some Evidence/Evident.

- Do a walkabout with at least one other to take stock.

- Assess the overall strengths and gaps.

- Identify what needs to change: What's next?

- Refresh or improve your knowledge and understanding of greening.

After taking stock at the cottage you will be thinking about what needs to change. You are reminded, too, to think mindfully about key ideas, or greening strategies. Greening strategies are the principles of greening, or targets, to ponder as projects and actions are considered. What do you think you know about the following?

- Conserving nature

- Energy efficiency

- Renewable resources

- Eco-friendly materials

- Reducing greenhouse gases

- Sustainable lifestyle practices

Reflect upon your current knowledge and understanding of these strategies, and what you think you will need to learn next to improve your greening habits or practices.

The greening practices which follow consistently appear in environmental publications, on green websites, and are visible on many of the product labels in retail outlets.

# 2. Four Rs and Beyond

It would be remiss to assume that the Four Rs: reuse, repair, reduce, and recycle would be all there is to know and do to work toward a sustainable lifestyle. "Recycle" was once a comprehensive buzzword often synonymous with greening. We now know that there is more to greening than recycling.

A wealth of scientific information not only keeps us well informed about the vulnerable state of the environment, but what we can do to improve it. Understanding the inherent need to conserve energy, select renewable resources and eco-friendly materials, to reduce greenhouse gases, and to live consciously with nature in mind, will guide the way to sustainable lifestyle practices which include the four Rs and beyond. Practically speaking, greening practices involve:

- Reclaiming, restoring, and repurposing eco-friendly objects and materials.

- Conserving water and energy.

- Investing in eco-friendly materials, renewable resources, and energy-efficient upgrades.

- Minimizing "stuff"!

It is important to consider society's compulsion for collecting stuff, and its impact upon the environment. For too long, we have forgotten the simple and sustainable practices of our grandparents. A throwaway and wasteful attitude has been adopted with the presumed need for convenience and gathering of stuff. Landfill sites are overburdened with our trash, and are now off-gassing harmful greenhouse gases into the air and leaching offensive chemicals into our water systems.

Waste management is a costly and challenging enterprise in our communities. The excessive accumulation of waste in landfill sites is a direct result of too much stuff, and too little consideration for the destructive impact of our trash on the environment. How could a minimalist lifestyle affect greening? Think mindfully before you decide upon your next purchase:

- Do we really need it?

- How long will it last?

- Can it be multipurposed?

- Can it be repaired?

- Can it eventually be recycled?

Within the context of what needs to change at the cottage, conscious decision-making will be grounded in your knowledge and understanding of a number of common greening practices.

## 2.1 Common greening practices

We know that greening practices extend beyond the Four Rs. There are several greening practices which describe interrelated actions that all focus on restoring a sustainable environment. With what we know today, greening practices should be commonplace. The following practices will serve as a reminder — food for thought — of what needs to happen in our daily lives.

### 2.1a Reuse and repair

Reusing and repairing reduces the amount of recyclables and ultimately minimizes refuse bound for landfill sites. The first recourse to sustainable waste management must be to reuse, rather than to recycle or discard.

Repair or refurbish well-made items so that they can be reused or repurposed. The following are ways which you can reuse common items and articles in good repair or that are repairable, thus reducing the amount of recyclables in the system:

- Save glass, plastic, and tin containers for storage of such products as foodstuffs and homemade cleaners.

- Refinish stored away antiques to once again serve a functional purpose.

- Use cloth table napkins/linens. Check out Grandma's linen closet, or go shopping at thrift shops or garage sales.

- Treat your baby to cloth diapers (provided you have an adequate water supply for the additional laundry).

- Purchase, in the first place, quality reusable and repairable goods!

## 2.1b Reclaim and salvage

You can reclaim or salvage quality building materials, unique fixtures, and ornate hardware and objects to prevent them from going to the landfill, and to add artful character to your cottage. Reclaimed wood from an old house or cottage, for example, is likely to be of old-growth forest wood, a much denser and better quality product than today's newer growth stock. And, salvaging ornamental door handles, broken crockery, or scrap-tile need not be overlooked for artistic creations and decorative features at the cottage. Sources for reclaimed and salvaged resources and materials are:

- Demolition sites when a building is being torn down.

- Local "re-store" facilities or other retail services where reclaimed building materials, fixtures, and goods are collected and sold.

- Thrift shops.

- Garage sales.

- At home: Check your own garage, basement, or attic. You may have forgotten about that beautiful walnut library cart gifted from Aunt Jane's estate, waiting to serve as your cottage bookshelf.

## 2.1c Repurpose

Find a new use for an object, or product. Whether you decide on a new function for keeping your china teacups useful, or, to use ingredients from the kitchen cupboard for your next cleaning job, repurposing can be a lot of fun and very satisfying. Repurposing includes:

- Relocating to the cottage a piece of furniture which one just cannot part with, yet no longer fits the decor at home.

- Accessorizing the garden with a china teacup and saucer bird feeder, or an old wooden ladder trellis — basically using objects for different purposes than they were intended.

- Using common ingredients found in the kitchen cupboard such as vinegar to make eco-friendly household cleaners (more about cleaners in section 3.3). Did you know that the baking soda in your kitchen cupboard is an eco-friendly multipurpose cleaner? In addition to its baking qualities, baking soda can:

  - Eliminate refrigerator odors. Keep an open box in your fridge.

  - Remove stains from fabrics and upholstery. Mix with a little water to form a paste and work into the stain with a soft cloth or toothbrush. Launder as usual, or let dry on upholstery and brush off.

  - Scrub greasy pots and pans. Mix with a little dish detergent and rub vigorously over the greasy surface with a cloth or sponge.

  - Clean your teeth. Use as a tooth powder to brush your teeth.

  - Soften hard water. Add ¼ cup baking soda to the laundry washer.

## 2.1d Multipurpose

Multipurposing is where creativity comes into play. Multipurposing takes a minimalist approach where the utility of an object can serve a dual purpose. Multipurposing will reduce the "stuff" at the cottage and inevitably the trash at the landfill site. Think about how something can serve more than one purpose, such as:

- A metal ash pail doubling as a firewood or kindling holder.

- A stainless steel pail sharing the chores as a water bucket, and a storage container for cleaning or garden supplies.

- A clay wine cooler for holding long-handled kitchen utensils and tools.

## 2.1e  Reduce

Reduce the carbon footprint with these mindful moves:

- Shop locally.

- Buy in bulk.

- Plan purchases or replacement of large appliances so that one delivery can be made, and at the same time if possible one removal trip.

- Hire local tradespersons.

- Plan errands so that they can all be taken care of in one trip.

- Bike to the market, walk to the beach, jog to the mailbox, kayak to the neighbor's! Find ways to not drive.

## 2.1f  Recycle

Recycling is to re-form or change something from one state into another in order to reuse it. Plastic bottles can be recycled into a synthetic fabric used to make fleece jackets; aluminum cans can become cookware, wire, automobile parts (just to name a few possibilities); and, kitchen and garden waste decomposes, or recycles, into rich compost to add to the soil in planting pots and gardens. In many areas, recycling will be part of your community waste management program or services. Always keep abreast with what is happening with your local recycling program because it is in constant flux as more is being learned about recycling and recyclables. Materials which can be recycled in most locales include:

- Non-glossy paper.

- Cartons and cereal boxes.

- Corrugated cardboard.

- Glass.

- Aluminum cans.

- Plastic containers.

And remember, composting is recycling your kitchen, garden, and yard plant refuse right at the cottage! (More about composting in section 3.2.)

## 2.1g Removal

Removal of an object or material must happen in some situations; not everything can be reused, repurposed, or recycled. Some materials and hazardous waste products will have to be disposed of in a safe way. Hazardous materials can generally be dropped off at depots specializing in their safe removal.

In some rural areas, burning refuse is a common practice for removal. Burning, however, releases hazardous gases into the environment, as well as creates fire safety issues in your neighborhood. It is important to check with your local fire department to know what materials can and cannot be burned, when the burning season is in effect, and what regulations on burning exist in your locale. No matter where you are located, burning the following common materials should be avoided at all costs: particle board and plywood (manufactured with toxic glues), treated and painted wood, garbage, plastics, glossy paper, and salted driftwood. These materials need to be taken to your local hazardous waste depot for safe removal.

Safe removal of refuse will differ from locale to locale. Check out what services for the removal of hazardous wastes are available in your community. Carefully determine how you will manage such waste materials and items as:

- Plastic containers from the garden and garage.

- Hard plastics such as broken lawn chairs, garden tools, and children's toys.

- Packaging from new purchases. Have you considered removing excessive packaging from appliances, tools, etc., at the point of purchase or not purchasing the items which are over-packaged? Perhaps this will cause manufacturers and retailers to minimize this extravagant disservice to our waste management services and environment.

- Toxic products from the bathroom, garden, and garage.

- Leftover paint.

- Dead and diseased plant debris, and noxious weeds from around the cottage property. (In some locales, these materials can be burned. Be sure to check the burning regulations where you are.)

- Used oils.

- Batteries from automobiles, boats, golf carts, or devices.

- Scrap and leftover building materials.

- Derelict hot water tanks, furnaces, fixtures, appliances, etc.

## 2.1h  Conserve natural resources

Conserve resources at the cottage, particularly water and energy. Conscious stewards of the environment work at conserving water by:

- Repairing leaking taps and pipes.

- Installing low-flow shower heads and dual flush toilets, or checking out the municipal guidelines on a composting or electric toilet.

- Placing a bucket in the shower to catch the water, and then pouring the water onto the garden.

- Replacing old clothes washers and dishwashers with High Efficiency (HE) appliances.

- Landscaping with drought tolerant native plants that will not require watering.

- Washing vegetables in a bowl of water rather than in the sink; pour the dirty water (called grey water) onto plants. Did you know that grey water can make up to 50–80 percent of your cottage waste water?

- Catching rainwater for watering plants, washing the windows and the car, or for an outdoor shower.

- Using a water cup rather than running the tap for brushing teeth. Did you know that when you use a cup of water to brush your teeth you can save approximately 12 liters or 3.17 gallons of water a day?

- Using microfiber cleaning cloths (their densely packed fibers reduce and conserve water usage).

They also work at conserving electricity or energy by:

- Upgrading electrical wiring in older cottages to current standards (check this out with an electrician).

- Insulating water pipes and the hot water tank. Did you know that by insulating your hot water tank you can reduce heat loss by 25–45 percent, and, lower your water heating costs by approximately 7–16 percent? Pipe wraps and tank blankets are easily fitted, inexpensive, and readily available at most hardware and home building retailers.

- Assessing the insulation factor in the cottage walls, floor, and roof, and upgrading to an R-value appropriate for the geographic area.

- Monitoring energy usage to plan where energy consumption can be reduced.

- Adding an auxiliary energy-efficient wood heating appliance and a renewable wood supply from a certified wood lot; or one's own trees which are windfallen or hazardous. (See Chapter 5 for more about efficient and clean wood heating.)

- Unplugging appliances when away or closing up the cottage for the season. Even standby mode on the TV consumes energy!

- Transitioning to energy efficient LED lighting and Energy Star appliances.

- Installing motion sensor lighting for outdoors.

- Investing in an alternative energy source such as geothermal, solar, or wind.

- Nurturing the "lights out" habit with the kids.

- Installing a DIY clothesline.

Salvage or reuse an aluminum umbrella clothesline and save energy by hanging the laundry outdoors to dry. (See Figure 2.)

What you will need:

- A used or salvaged aluminum umbrella clothesline/dryer, or, purchase one at the local hardware if necessary

- PVC pipe

- Metal bands

- Deck screws

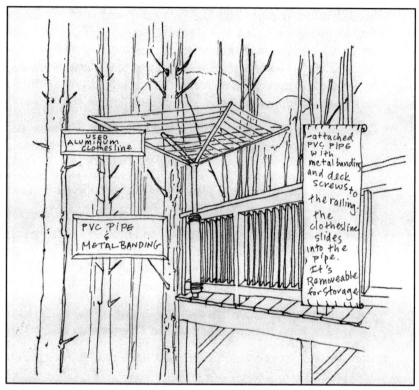

Figure 2: A DIY Clothesline

A clothesline is an opportunity to track your energy consumption as well as your energy bills. Compare usage and costs between two summer and two winter months (assuming you do not hang laundry outdoors during the winter). What is the difference in energy consumption between the two seasons? What are you saving in costs? And, you can easily remove the clothesline for winter storage or a summer deck party!

You will notice that common greening practices vary somewhat from source to source, locale to locale, and cottager to cottager. There is often overlap as well. Reusing and recycling may seem like the same action at your cottage. Ultimately, both actions are acts of kindness with nature in mind. However they are referenced, they are both greening actions which will prevent something from ending up in the landfill and possibly off-gassing harmful toxins into the air we breathe and the water we drink. Within the scope of these common greening practices, we have the knowledge and the capability to change destructive human lifestyle habits.

Rethinking these practices will refresh and may even add to your knowledge base, and should offer clearer insights to your goal(s) and plans.

## 2.2 Common greening practices and furnishing your cottage

At the same time as you are refreshing and reflecting upon your understanding of common greening practices, some of your first plans may be involving the furnishing of your cottage. Particularly, if you have just purchased or built a new cottage, it is likely that you will be needing furniture and kitchenware within a relatively short time. This means you will have an immediate opportunity to begin furnishing your cottage in an environmentally conscious way.

If, for example, you are intent on reducing your GHGs at your cottage, you will likely consider shopping locally as much as possible. Your "shopping," too, may include thrifting, going to garage sales, and checking at home for eco-friendly repairable furniture and accessories no longer in use. You may find yourself repairing, reusing, repurposing, and multipurposing to prevent eco-friendly items from home going to a landfill site. It is probable that you will have some new purchases to make, too. When making new purchases, think about quality items that will last and which are constructed from renewable resources and/or eco-friendly materials. Wood, stainless steel, iron, pottery/earthenware, glass, and natural fabrics are sustainable materials which will add to the décor of your cottage as well as provide practical and functional furnishings, kitchenware, and accessories. (For substantive purchases such as large appliances, see Chapter 5, section 2.1c on the replacement or purchase of major appliances.)

When we purchased our cottage, we had no furnishings or accessories. We had to immediately plan how we would furnish our cottage in an environmentally conscious way. Thrifting was our first mission, and it was a lot of fun! With four metal folding chairs, glass canisters for food storage, iron fire place accessories, stainless kitchen cutlery, utensils, pots and pans, unique pieces of crockery, table linens, and a couple of table lamps, we were able to begin practicing our cottage greening lifestyle. Much of our eclectic cottage furnishings also came from our homes: antique chairs, Petit Point china, a wooden library cart, and a wicker table and chairs.

Figure 3: Furnishing our cottage

If you have a furnished cottage, then furnishings, kitchenware, and accessories will be part of your taking stock exercise. Is your furniture, for example, reflective of the Four Rs and Beyond: reclaiming, restoring/repairing, reusing, repurposing, multipurposing, and, minimizing "stuff"?

Now, you may want to do some further research on a specific greening practice which has an immediate need for action at your cottage.

# 3. What's Next? A Practical Project

Having taken stock, do you now notice any gaps or contradictions between your current practices and habits, and your greening vision?

Have you discovered something that needs to happen sooner rather than later? Do you need to know more about eco-friendly and biodegradable products and materials? Are you now convinced to practice composting? Revelations such as these are cues for taking on a practical project.

A practical project is an action that is a direct result of taking stock and a prerequisite, or "pre-action," to developing one's Cottage Greening Action Plan. A practical project is, in fact, learning in action to determine what one currently knows, and what new learning and knowledge is necessary to move forward.

Reflecting upon your taking stock exercise, choose a practical project which you and your fellow cottagers can explore and learn more about. Consider practicing and reflecting upon the four Rs: reuse, repurpose, reduce, or recycle; perhaps painting the deck, for example, may be of interest to you right now. Exploring and starting a practical project will help you discover what you already know, and what new learning you will need in order to work toward practicing your greening vision. Consider these tips when choosing your practical project:

A practical project —

- is affordable; it can even be free,

- has some immediacy to it,

- is learning in action,

- has short-term observable results, e.g., composting or decreasing your volume of recyclables will have observable results within 9—12 months,

- includes the support and knowledge of your family or fellow cottagers, and

- requires collective reflection on how you are going towards your greening vision.

The following practical projects offer an opportunity for exploring and learning at the same time. These projects will be pre-actions to facilitate the development of your Cottage Greening Action Plan (See Chapter 4). Choose a practical project which seems to connect best with your greening vision and current needs, and with one of the gaps uncovered in your taking stock exercise.

## 3.1 Painting, inside and out

When painting, choose eco-friendly materials to renew and conserve exterior and interior building materials, finishes, fixtures, objects, and accessories. Painting today will also cover yesteryear's old lead-based paints, which are highly toxic.

What you will need to know: Common paint manufacturers have a good variety of eco-friendly "green" paints, paint cleaners, and tack cloth. Low- and no-Volatile Organic Compounds (VOC) paints and stains, and certified products free from off-gassing carcinogens and toxins, are available on the shelves of many retailers. Most eco-friendly paint can be cleaned up with water and a small quantity of dish detergent. This goes for cleaning the brushes and rollers, too. If an oil-based product is used, you can clean up with a citrus solvent rather than turpentine.

What you will need to do:

• Read labels to find eco-friendly product(s).

• Purchase just enough paint for the project.

• Prepare to paint using eco-friendly products for cleaning the surface, edging, etc. If mold exists, find the source of the moisture and repair the problem first. Do not paint over mold.

• Wrap brushes and rollers in plastic between coats. Did you know that your brushes and rollers can be wrapped in plastic and popped into the freezer if a few days are going to lapse before getting back to the project?

• Clean brushes or rollers, when finished, with water, or with a citrus solvent if an oil-based paint or stain was used.

• Properly dispose of leftover paint; check if the local waste management service has a paint recycling program. If just a little paint is left over, add kitty litter to harden it. Then, dispose as a household hazardous waste.

The results are obvious: your cottage will be clean and fresh, and you will have given new life to something which may have been heading to the landfill site. You will also have extended the life of the building and finishing materials at the cottage. What is not obvious is that your cottage will be free of toxic paint odors, and off-gassing. It will be a healthy place for you, and for the environment.

Take note of the amount of paint used for the project, and of the color number. Painting projects are generally cyclic, and having this information on hand will be useful.

## 3.2 Composting

Reducing greenhouse gases, recycling kitchen and garden trash, minimizing landfill pollution, and creating a valuable gardening product — rich brown compost — is a direct result of composting.

You will need a compost bin or a garden area to build a compost pile; kitchen vegetable and fruit waste, teabags, coffee grounds, eggshells; garden and yard trimmings, and leaves and grass clippings; nonglossy paper products, compostable egg cartons and cereal boxes (cut into smaller pieces); and wood ashes. Avoid meat, dairy, baby diapers, and animal feces as they smell, attract pests, and may harbor harmful bacteria. Composting requires moisture, oxygen, and warmth (sunny locations help decomposition).

What you will need to do:

- Create a compost pile or choose a bin. You could drill some holes into the sides and bottom of a lidded steel garbage can or make a cylinder of chicken wire or similar.

- Layer your compostable materials according to wet and dry layers.

- Sprinkle lightly with soil every three to four layers.

- Keep slightly moist and turn or mix composting materials every two to three weeks.

- Watch, over 9–12 months, the work of soil creatures and microbes as the biodegradable materials rot and turn into compost.

- Add the dark rotted compost from the bottom of the compost bin, or pile, to your pots and garden.

What do you smell? A bad smell should not be coming from your compost! If a bad smell is noticeable, adjust the thickness of the layers and the addition of moisture. These variables will differ depending upon your climate, and the season. Air, too, needs to be able to flow through the decomposing materials. Add egg cartons and crumpled newspaper to create air pockets which enable healthy composting. Did you remember not to add meat and dairy waste to the compost bin or pile?

Check for any materials which are not breaking down. For example, stickers on store-bought fruits and vegetables will not decompose; they need to be removed before items are added into the compost bin or pile. Take notes so that you can refine your composting process.

## 3.3 Homemade cleaning products

Many products and ingredients from the kitchen cupboards or pantry can be repurposed as environmentally-safe cleaning products. White vinegar, cream of tartar, baking soda, table and Epsom salts, and hydrogen peroxide (3 percent) are most commonly used for cutting grease and for non-abrasive scrubbing around the cottage. For example, tea stains are easily and safely removed from cups and teapots with a thin paste of baking soda or a sprinkling of table salt. Begin making your own eco-friendly homemade cleaning products.

Homemade cleaners conserve nature by reducing the toxins which contaminate our water and air, and by reducing the amount of plastic spray bottles/containers bound for landfills.

What you will need to do: Search your kitchen and pantry for the ingredients called for in the following recipes, mix as directed, and store any leftover homemade products in used, reusable bottles and containers. Start cleaning.

What are you observing? Did you need to make any adjustments? What works best for you?

### 3.3a  Windows, kitchen, and bathroom counters

Use a solution of two parts water, one part vinegar. Store in a reused spray bottle. Wipe windows dry and streak-free with newspaper.

### 3.3b  Bathroom shower, tub, sink cleaner, and mold remover

Mix one teaspoon liquid dish soap, two to three drops of antibacterial oil such as lemongrass or thyme, and a small amount of water. Clean away soap scum and water spots.

### 3.3c Oven

Mix together a paste of baking soda and vinegar. Apply paste to oven walls, top, and bottom. Wipe or sponge off after five to ten minutes. Leave overnight if cleaning an extra greasy oven.

### 3.3d Barbecue grill

Cut an onion in half; attach it to a fork or skewer. Rub it across a hot grill grate. Your grate will be clean and sweetly flavored.

### 3.3e Stain remover

Mix one part liquid dish soap to two parts hydrogen peroxide (3 percent). Store in a reused spray bottle. Spray onto stain, and launder.

### 3.3f Kettle hard water scale remover

Hard water causes a buildup of scale in your kettle. All you need to remove this white, flaky lime accumulation is vinegar. In your kettle, bring to a boil equal parts vinegar and water. Remove your kettle from the heat and let it sit overnight. The next day empty the kettle and rinse thoroughly with fresh water. Did you know that running the rinse cycle of the dishwasher with the addition of a cup of white vinegar will remove hard water buildup in your dishwasher, too?

### 3.3g Septic tank activator/conditioner

To initiate or enhance the bacteria count in your septic tank — and to eliminate odor, you will need:

- 454 grams / 1 lb. brown sugar
- 1 liter/quart hot water
- 10 ml / 2 teaspoons dry yeast

Thoroughly mix the brown sugar in hot water and cool to luke-warm. Stir in yeast, and when dissolved flush down the toilet.

## 3.4 Reduce recyclables

Reducing the trash which your local waste management service regularly picks up from your cottage will reduce the amount of trash in your community's landfill, and ultimately reduce the emission of toxic greenhouse gases into the atmosphere.

What you will need to do: Find out exactly what is recyclable in your community. Note the recycle icon on plastic containers such as yogurt tubs. Some recycle depots only accept certain classifications of plastics.

Begin sorting right in the kitchen. For example, set up a simple sorting system under the kitchen sink. See Figure 4.

If you have a recycling pick-up service in your community, follow the directions provided by this service provider.

If you do not have a pick-up service, set aside a place in your garden shed, or elsewhere, to hold the recyclables until you plan to deliver them to your community recycling depot. See Figure 5.

Drop off your recyclables at the recycling depot and take note of anything new on their notice board. Recycling is a constantly evolving process.

Figure 4: Recycling under the sink

Figure 5: Recycling in the shed

Figure 6: Recycling at the depot

Monitor your weekly volume of recyclables. Is the amount of recyclables decreasing?

## 3.5 Chemical-free pest control

Scientific evidence is clear that pesticides and insecticides are having a horrific environmental impact. These toxic chemicals are infiltrating our water and air.

As a result, a number of serious health threats to wildlife and to human life have been discovered. Pesticides and insecticides can:

- Compromise the immune system.
- Cause certain cancers.
- Effect a lowering of human sperm count.
- Kill countless numbers of birds and fish.

Cottagers have the responsibility to control pests without using chemicals and poisons. Eco-friendly ways to control pests and to promote a healthy environment for humankind and nature are paramount.

Conserve nature by using eco-friendly products which reduce the toxins that contaminate our water and air and have a harmful impact upon the health of humans and wildlife. This will ensure that our children, pets, and neighborhood wildlife are not harmed by coming into direct contact with poisons.

What you will need to do: First off, avoid any invitation to pests. Rodents, ants, fleas, mosquitoes, weevils, flour beetles, clothing moths, house flies, and wasps are some common pests which will take haven at the cottage if the opportunity is right. Also, read labels with care if you are shopping for commercial eco-friendly products to control household and garden pests.

To safely control the pests at your cottage, inside and out:

- Store food in tightly sealed glass or tin containers.
- Screen windows and porches.
- Fly swatting works. Do you know that every fly swatted will prevent several hundred from hatching?
- Use natural and biodegradable pesticides. Diatomaceous earth (horticultural grade for outdoors or food grade for indoors), is

an excellent product for killing insects such as fleas, ants, and pill bugs. The sharp edges of these desiccating dusts cut the insects' body coverings. Thus, the insects die from dehydration.

- Use snap traps, not poison, to control rodents. Or, bring your cat to the cottage to take care of the rodents.

- Mix oils such as lemongrass, mint, lavender, bay laurel, or geranium with water to spray for garden pests.

- Spray indoor insects with a mixture of soap and water (2 tablespoons liquid dish soap in 4 liters/1 gallon of water). Even a wasp will succumb when directly sprayed with a soap and water solution.

- Store firewood away from the cottage to keep rodents, powder post beetles, termites, and carpenter ants at bay.

Wasps and yellowjackets have become extreme tormentors at many cottages, especially around the barbecue and picnic table. You will most likely have to deal with these pests at least once through the summer months.

Tips for controlling wasps:

- Keep garbage cans covered and away from the cottage.

- Prevent the start-up of a nest in springtime by knocking down last year's nest.

- Carefully remove active wasp nests at night, enclosing them with a paper bag, and then submerging into soapy water.

- Wear dull colors and avoid perfume.

- Stay calm and move slowly.

- Feed pets inside rather than outdoors.

- Use a fly swatter around the picnic table.

- Purchase or make a wasp trap.

## 3.5a How to make a wasp trap

What you will need to do to make a wasp trap:

- Get a milk jug or water bottle, with a cap.

- Cut a small entrance hole near the top. You do not want the bees to escape through this hole.

- Partially fill with apple juice, soda pop, or a light coating of jam.

- Hang your trap away from the picnic tables and any sitting area(s).

- To empty, drop the trap into soapy water. This will kill the bees.

Hopefully, your pests will no longer be pestering you. Observe and note what is working and what is not working. Creatures are wise and can become wary of our control measures. In extreme situations, call an exterminator who has the expertise to deal safely with chemicals if this should be the only recourse.

Beyond the cottage, take time to observe the merchandising of pesticides at your local retail outlet. When we refrain from purchasing toxic products and treatments, more eco-friendly products will stock the shelves. Are you noticing an eco-friendly shift where you shop?

### 3.5b An environmental note about pests

It would be remiss not to draw one's attention to the fact that most pests around the cottage serve an integral role in environmental sustainability. Bees, ants, bats, and flies may become pests when they get into, or live too close to, the cottage. However, each species provides a necessary role in maintaining a healthy environment. Ironically, in nature these predators and prey control our cottage pests. In this regard, our cottage pests are also our friends.

# 4. Now That You've Taken Stock and Started a Practical Project, What's Next?

Finally, taking stock makes way for greening possibilities and practicalities at the cottage. A practical project takes care of an imminent need, serves a useful greening purpose, and becomes a learning experience in itself. A practical project can draw our attention to what we think we know, and what we will need to know and to learn, in order to move forward. Adjust your Taking Stock checklist as needed.

The next chapter will take a closer look at becoming environmentally savvy as you go about greening your cottage, inside and out.

# 3
# Becoming Environmentally Savvy

*We now know from endless scientific studies that we are actively destroying the only planet we know that can sustain us.*

— Sheherazade Goldsmith

Becoming environmentally savvy is an ongoing journey for everyone at the cottage. Science is constantly uncovering new findings, both hopeful and despairing. In keeping well-informed in current environmental research, and acting in accordance with what is known, there is hope.

Concern for nature affects us all. The introduction of chemicals, non-biodegradable materials, and so-called convenience has seriously impeded, and even destroyed in some instances, nature. We now question too, within our technological lives, devices, cell phones, routers, microwave ovens, smart meters in some areas — how radioactive and electromagnetic emissions might further threaten nature's work, and our own health.

Some species, such as birds and honeybees, are suffering from the proliferation of electromagnetic fields which interlace their habitat. Honeybees, for example, have been known to leave their colonies where high levels of electromagnetic emissions exist. With the loss of these pollinators in our gardens, we are not only losing local honey supplies, but also the bounty of vegetables, fruits, and flowers. Because of unconscious human intervention, the air we breathe, the water we drink, and the space in which we live often contain harmful contaminants and emissions which adversely affect human health. Flora and fauna have been put at risk, too. Some species have even become extinct.

There is hope, however, even within consciously eco-friendly actions at the cottage. With the scientific research and knowledge that you have access to today, and as you learn from exploring a variety of greening practices, you can make a difference.

Daily greening acts, such as cleaning with ingredients from the kitchen cupboard, or, a substantive project to retrofit an open fireplace with a clean technology such as a catalytic stove, will make a positive difference. When putting eco-friendly actions into practice, learning is inevitable and necessary. There is much that can happen when you have an openness to learning and to recognizing what needs to be known about greening.

However your learning and actions toward your greening vision unfold, you have the capabilities to be an active agent, or steward, in working towards a sustainable environment.

# 1. Living an Environmentally Sustainable Lifestyle Is Not New

I remember the everyday environmental consciousness of Mom and Grannie. Water conservation was evident when our clothes were washed, whites through darks, in a wringer washer which reused the same water, load after load. And then the grey water flowed out onto the garden. Grannie's homemade laundry soap did an excellent job at cleaning grass-stained pants, and was kinder to nature.

Biodegradable ingredients were used to clean the windows. Water, vinegar, and newspaper resulted in clean windows with a streakless shine. The waxed inner bags from cereal boxes were reused to keep our lunchbox sandwiches fresh, or to wrap a leftover from dinner. Kitchen waste was dug into the garden soil without us ever talking about composting.

I also remember when convenience superseded consciousness: commercially produced detergents replaced Grannie's homemade laundry soap; upon moving from the country, city garbage pickup replaced our compost pile; flannelette diapers lovingly sewn by my Mom gave way to disposables (only when we were traveling!); and food, in all sorts of plastics and from all corners of the world, replaced our own homegrown, organic garden produce. ("Organic" was not part of our vocabulary, either.) The results of convenience have had a devastating impact upon nature and our environment.

Greening at the cottage reminds me of growing up with a simpler eco-friendly lifestyle. Greening at the cottage, inside and out, brings forth hope. I am hopeful that with today's modelling of an enduring commitment to greening, my family and future generations, wherever they reside, will once again choose an environmentally sustainable lifestyle.

Rethinking current practices and the ways of our grandparents brings to light a simpler and more practical approach to greening. With your greening vision as a guide, numerous ways to deepen your understanding of how a sustainable environment looks, sounds, and feels can be sought.

## 2. What Do You Need to Know about Greening at the Cottage?

First off, you need to remember that greening is not new. Previous generations practiced a simpler environmentally sustainable lifestyle. Think about your current greening habits. Rethink where you can make adjustments and improvements to move your ultimate greening vision forward.

Second, you need to know that greening is a shared responsibility. Everyone at the cottage is responsible for and integral to making your greening vision a reality. In fact, it is assumed that your greening vision was crafted with the input of all family members or cottagers. Third, listen to the kids. Children have an innate connection to nature, and a developing theoretical understanding of environmental sustainability through their schools' curricula. Ask them what they know about taking care of the environment. How can they work towards a healthier environment for ourselves and for all of nature's plants and animals? How can they put their learning and understanding into action at the cottage? The cottage, whether surrounded by nature, or with nature close by, is the perfect place to put theory into practice.

Finally, realize that you can make a difference with a growing knowledge, a deepening understanding, and consistent mindful practice. Practicing what you know today will inform you as to what you need to know tomorrow in order to hone your greening practices. You are on a greening journey.

# 3. Learning and Greening

Learning and greening go hand in hand. Informal learning is inevitable when going for a walk, noticing the beauty and wonders of the flora and fauna.

Daily greening practices such as composting and reducing waste and recyclables are acts of kindness with nature in mind, or, practical projects towards sustainability. A formal learning opportunity may be enrolling in a workshop about renewable resources for sustainable renovations, or, how to go about increasing your cottage's insulation R-value and decreasing your energy consumption and costs. Ongoing learning, whether informal or formal, is integral to your greening commitment.

It is important that everyone understands and values the cottage greening vision and how it will guide the ongoing learning journey. Be alert to what learning opportunities are available for the kids and the adults in your cottage community. The learning opportunities detailed in the next sections explore and suggest practical and engaging ways to:

- Learn about nature and the environment.

- Practice greening at the cottage.

- Deepen our understanding of a sustainable lifestyle.

Figure 7: Learning

## 3.1 Nature's classroom for tomorrow's stewards

*Children are born with a sense of wonder and an affinity for Nature. Properly cultivated, these values can mature into ecological literacy, and eventually into sustainable patterns of living.*

— Zenobia Barlow, "Confluence of Streams"

Stewardship is about appreciating and taking care of nature, and demonstrating responsible actions to conserve our natural resources and the environment. When the cottage is surrounded in the beauty and awe of nature, there is a natural calling for children and adults to explore and to interact with nature. This is a prime opportunity to learn about and to practice living in harmony with nature. The outdoors provides the classroom and a hands-on, minds-on learning experience.

Even if the cottage is not surrounded by nature, it is important to know that stewardship will positively impact the surroundings, wherever the cottage.

Nature's classroom provides a link between the theory learned in classrooms at school, and the experiences happening at the cottage. Learning happens when exploring your property and neighborhood, learning about the deer, ants, raccoons, frogs, ravens, sea stars, butterflies, and bees. There are also those critters who can't be seen as they are hard at work in the decaying compost, living high above in the forest canopy, or are camouflaged in the ferns. Scavenger hunts, sketching and painting, cottage chores, building a bird house, writing stories, planning daily cottage activities, and reading great children's literature about the environment are all rich learning experiences. Learning nurtures curiosity, extends understanding, initiates responsibility, and fosters stewardship.

Reading children's literature, whether in nature's classroom, or by the fire on a rainy day, fosters an appreciation for and a deeper understanding of nature and conservation. Learning that they have a responsibility to be avid stewards of the environment is fun, meaningful, and motivating; children are ready and eager to take action.

Some of our favorite children's reads on our bookshelves at the cottage (and at home) are listed on the download kit included with this book. And, don't forget a trip to the local library: This is an opportunity to get into some great environmental books and to see how books can be shared in order to reduce, reuse, and even recycle.

Figure 8: Forest Management

## 3.2 Learning and practicing stewardship with the kids

Learning and greening with the kids will ultimately foster stewardship; a deep appreciation of and an inherent responsibility to nature. This important learning is enhanced at the cottage not only because of a closer proximity to nature, but also because parents will have more time to spend with the kids.

Within this opportune learning environment, it is important to remember that children learn what they see and hear. They learn from the actions of the significant adults in their lives. Greening at the cottage is an ideal opportunity to explore firsthand the forest or land, to think about a clean and sufficient water supply, and to become perceptive of energy resources, such as electricity or off-grid alternatives. And, all this rich learning can be practiced without a screen!

To foster stewardship at your cottage:

- Nurture or plant native trees to offer nesting sites and shelter for birds and bats, perches for songbirds, food for moths, shade for animals and cottagers, and a sturdy branch for the kids' swing or for your hammock.

- Pile windfallen branches, sticks, and logs on the ground to create habitat for creatures such as bugs, spiders, flies, and toads, and all those critters too small to see.

- Plant a native ground cover such as ferns, sedum, or a long native grass such as California fescue to eliminate grass mowing and to provide moist conditions and shelter for frogs, toads, and ground beetles.

- Plan a low-maintenance rock garden, or a space to grow or naturalize nectar-producing flowers such as daisies, wild asters, violas, or sunflowers for foraging bees and butterflies.

- Leave seed heads on grasses and flowers for seed-eaters such as finches and chickadees.

- Build a birdhouse or a bat house with the kids, inspiring them to nurture nature. Did you know that during one night, a bat may eat up to 3,000 mosquitoes?

- Read aloud *Night Tree*, by Eve Bunting, and decorate a celebration tree for the critters and creatures at your cottage. Who will come? Who will favor what?

## 3.3 Simple rainwater catchments

With the adverse effects of climate change and pollution, water is no longer considered a renewable resource in many parts of the world. This is so in cottage country, too. In fact, for many cottagers, water restrictions have become a way of managing a declining water supply. For these reasons, many cottagers are considering simple rainwater catchments. A simple water catchment system is:

- Easy to install. There are even DIY kits available in local retail outlets.

- A good supplementary supply of non-drinking water for lawns and gardens, and limited domestic use such for handwashing, showering, and laundry.

- A way to conserve both water and energy.

Rainwater catchment, whether the cottage is situated in a rainforest or on the plains, is becoming an important means of water conservation. For most cottagers, rainwater is a supplemental supply of water rather than the primary water source. Even where rainfall is minimal, rainwater catchment will reduce the water consumption from a municipal/local water source, or, from one's own well supply. This reduction in water consumption protects the aquifer; that is, it helps to sustain the amount of surface water — from rain and melting snow — which is stored in the underground aquifer.

Rainwater catchment can be as simple as a rain barrel situated by the cottage, or it can involve a sophisticated system: catchment, filtration, storage, purification, pumping, and chilling if the water is to be potable. Most cottages can easily support a simple rainwater catchment system. Materials and supplies are readily available at building supply outlets, many hardware stores, and authorized water catchment/harvesting dealers. Simple rainwater catchment involves/requires:

- A roof.

- Gutters and downspouts.

- Leaf catcher/strainers (optional).

- Storage barrel(s) or holding tank(s).

- A pump if the water is being used for domestic purposes.

The basis of simple rainwater collection is the collection surface, generally the cottage roof, and gravity. The pitch and roofing material make a difference to the quantity and quality of the water collected. For example, a steel or metal roof is more efficient than a roof finished with cedar shakes or asphalt shingles. Generally, with a metal roof, there will be more water and fewer contaminants. If you are interested in calculating the amount of rainwater which could be collected from your cottage roof, there are a variety of websites and formulae available. One website which you may find helpful is http://rainwaterharvesting.tamu.edu/calculators/.

If gutters and downspouts are not already installed on your cottage roof, this can be a DIY project, or one where a professional roofer or gutter installer is contracted. Even where gutters are already a part of the cottage roof system, they may not have any protection from debris such as leaves. Leaf catchers or leaf strainers are readily available at building material outlets and are suitable for new or existing gutters. It is recommended that gutters are equipped with strainers to minimize debris and contaminants, which over time can clog your gutters and downspouts, and create a build-up of organic materials and unwanted bacteria in your storage barrel or holding tank.

Storage barrels and holding tanks come in a wide variety of materials, shapes, and sizes; however, most tanks at the cottage are poly. Gravity is generally the primary means of directing the rainwater from the roof to the barrel or tank, and to the garden. A rain barrel may be located next to the cottage, preferably out of the direct sun, or, a holding tank may be housed in a water system shed in close proximity to the cottage. In some instances, the holding tank can be dug into the ground and a pumping system is an additional part of the installation. The size of the holding tank is dependent primarily upon the amount of yearly rainfall and the size of the cottage roof. The amount of projected water consumption can also be a consideration when choosing a tank. A certified dealer can help you determine the best holding tank and site for your climate, ground conditions, space, and consumption needs.

If your cottage is in a location where rainwater will be your primary water source, you will need to seek professional assistance and/or a certified installer. Such systems for potable water are complex and generally best suited for new construction.

Did you know that simple rainwater catchment can generally reduce the water consumption from your primary source/supply by approximately 20–60 percent? Water conservation is an essential practice inside the cottage, and out.

## 3.4 Exploring the forest, or woods

Because the trees in our forest and woodlands clean the air of dangerous toxins as well as provide habitat and food for wildlife, we want our children to understand and to appreciate their important environmental role. How can kids take care of the forest, woodlands, or a tree? Ponder this on walks and scavenger hunts through the woods. Practice the power of observation: "How many creatures can you see?" "or hear?" This is another opportunity to use children's literature to learn to identify and name the local trees and wildlife. If a forest or woodland is not accessible at your cottage, plant a native tree, or trees, should space allow. Planting, observing, and caring for a tree is about conservation. And, with the practice of stewardship over the years, that tree will clean harmful $CO^2$ from the air, and offer safe shelter and an abundance of food to local wildlife. That tree will help to save energy, too, when its branches shade your cottage from the hot sun.

If such opportunities are not possible at your cottage, it is well worth taking a day trip to a nearby forest or woods. Bring along a couple of good books about local trees or animals that live in the forest; a camera or sketch pad; a bug jug; and some binoculars. Have fun!

## 3.5 Learning and conserving

Conservation is about the conscious acts taken to reduce consumption of a resource in order to sustain an adequate supply for all. Children, like the adults in their lives, are an integral part of the collective sustainable lifestyle at the cottage. The water supply, the energy source for lighting, heating, and cooking, and the increasing technologies at the cottage require prudent actions to conserve resources and to ensure the wellness of the cottagers and the environment.

Life at the cottage offers many opportunities for learning about and conserving water, energy, and reducing electromagnetic emissions, all of which will be discussed in the next sections.

## 3.5a  Conserving water

Water play is great fun! It is unlikely though, that any child will heed water conservation rules when playing with the garden hose on a hot summer's day, or taking an extended shower at the end of a hot day.

Remind children that water is necessary to sustain all life: plants, animals, creatures, critters, and people, too. Safe water is a natural resource which is becoming less and less renewable with climate change and pollution. Children need to know that much of the world's water supply has been contaminated with harmful toxins from the trash in landfill sites, the use of pesticides and herbicides, waste from manufacturing plants, and inadequate sanitation systems. Some cottagers are already experiencing a shortage of potable water and an inadequate water supply to sustain everyday living. As a result, many communities have water restrictions, particularly during the summer months. Help your child understand this. What would it be like to run out of water at the cottage? How can you and your child practice water conservation? Think about the common, everyday ways you can conserve water at your cottage:

- Use a cup of water when brushing teeth rather than running the tap.

- Flush the toilet mindfully (if a composting or electric toilet has not been installed).

- Shower quickly and turn off the water flow when applying soap or shampoo. Turn the water on again for rinsing.

- Shower outdoors with a bucket.

- Insert a portable dish pan into the kitchen sink for dishwashing. Pour the grey water onto a garden that is not close to the cottage because you do not want to attract pests with the food bits in the dish water.

- Wash vegetables and fruits in a bowl of water, and pour the grey water onto your garden or pots.

- Water the garden and wash the car with rainwater.

- Go to the beach rather than play in the sprinkler. There'll be more learning about nature, too!

- **Note:** Some jurisdictions allow for grey water disposal, usually water from the laundry, shower, and sometimes the kitchen sink, draining into a catchment tank or a drainage pit for reuse in the garden. Not all jurisdictions will permit grey water systems. The regulation of grey water systems varies according to different local sanitation regulations and must be carefully researched before considered for installation at your cottage.

Water conservation needs to be modelled by the adults in children's lives. When they understand the vital role water plays in sustaining all life — plants and animals, and people, too — children become conscious of how they can conserve water.

## 3.5b Saving energy

More choices for cleaner renewable energy resources such as wind, water, and solar are becoming available and more affordable with developing technologies. This is particularly evident with cottagers who choose an off-grid lifestyle, powering their cottages with renewable energy sources.

Electricity, however, prevails in many areas of the world, and there are still locales where electrical energy is sourced through coal rather than water. Coal-sourced electrical energy contributes to polluting the air with greenhouse gases. Once again, the commitment of the adults at the cottage will impact the actions of the children. Adults need to consciously and constantly model their greening actions for children to see and hear. Even the youngest child will take responsible action for saving energy when she consistently hears and sees a parent's "lights out" before walking out of a room or leaving the cottage. Though all tips which follow may not interest the kids per se, children are often intrigued with tracking data and consumption, and performing energy experiments which demonstrate the energy-saving principles involved. A wide variety of energy topics and experiments for children can be accessed on the Internet. (Visit the websites listed on the download kit for some engaging activities.)

Some ways to save energy:

- Insulate! Upgrade the insulation in the cottage floors, walls, and roof; wrap insulation around the hot water tank and hot water pipes; and maintain weather stripping for doors and windows. Check the recommended R-value for your climate or region.

- Unplug small appliances, devices, even chargers at the wall when away from the cottage. Did you know that even standby mode on the TV consumes energy?

- Launder full loads to conserve energy and water.

- Hang clothes to dry outdoors during fine weather.

- Install a rain barrel for an outdoor shower to conserve energy and water.

- Assess the need for air conditioning: Would a ceiling fan be more energy-efficient than air conditioning in your locale? What about large, screened windows for passive cooling as an alternative to AC?

- Invest in a solar powered, 12V battery charger to maintain, during the off-season, a trickle charge for your boat, all-terrain vehicle, snowmobile, or car batteries.

- Turn off the water heater when away from the cottage. Did you know that you can increase the efficiency and extend the life of your hot water heater by periodically draining the sedimentary build-up in the tank? (See Chapter 5 for more about how to drain a water heater or tank). Use motion detectors for outdoor lighting rather than leaving a light on all the time.

## 3.5c Minding electromagnetic emissions

For the health of our children and the well-being of the environment, plan to take a screen break when at the cottage. There is evidence that with a plethora of technology in our daily lives, we are constantly surrounded by the emissions of electromagnetic fields and radiation. Emissions are not only emanating from our devices, but also the technologies in many of today's appliances, entertainment systems, cordless phones, and smart meters, to mention just a few items. Though long-term effects of these emissions are not yet known, there is concern that electromagnetic emissions may be harmful to humans, and also to wildlife. Is that reason enough to spend less time looking at screens while at the cottage?

If less screen time is to be negotiated with the children, then they need to understand why. Furthermore, they need to know that the negotiated screen time applies to everyone at the cottage. If you take advantage of less screen time, you will have more time for learning;

particularly for learning about those critters outside, and ourselves. Managing electronic devices will be good for everyone at the cottage and for the health of the pollinators at work in the garden, too.

To reduce exposure to electromagnetic fields:

- Use LED lighting rather than compact fluorescent or incandescent bulbs.

- Assess whether you need a microwave, and other electromagnetic emitting systems at the cottage.

- Plan for, or schedule, less time on electronic devices.

- Hardwire the Internet rather than using a wireless connection.

- Turn off Wi-Fi when not in use.

- Keep chargers for devices out of the bedrooms.

- Have an old fashioned wind-up or battery-operated clock by your bedside.

Hope for moving towards a sustainable environment is imminent when children are active participants in greening. They become avid learners and potentially aspiring stewards as they experience firsthand what they can do to help with the greening at their cottage. Be sure that children see their contribution in the development of the Cottage Greening Action Plan, and their responsibility in its implementation (more on this in Chapter 4). Learning is empowering, and empowering children brings hope to working towards a sustainable lifestyle.

# 4. Deepening Understanding and Improving Your Greening Lifestyle

Clearly, there is much for all to learn. By gaining more knowledge and putting new learning into practice, a deeper understanding evolves. Whether learning is planned, or unplanned, formal or informal, there is great value in questioning and reflecting upon what you think you know, and, wondering and discovering with other like minds.

Become involved in a local environmental group or initiative, or a food group, or volunteer at a local recycling or hazardous waste depot. Listen and learn. Learn and practice. Practice and adjust. You will be able to question, share, and gain further insights about a practical project of interest, or something that you need to know to improve upon your greening lifestyle. Building upon and extending your knowledge base results in a deepening understanding. Understanding builds confidence: We can do this!

Reflect, too, on the various practical projects which are available right at the cottage. For example, if you are getting into composting, you will be exploring and learning as you go. Note that the kids can learn right alongside you! Think about how composting:

- Reduces the amount of trash you would be leaving for your local waste management service to deal with. It probably goes to a landfill site. And, what happens when it gets there?

- Reduces the carbon footprint, that is, the GHG emissions in the transporting of the kitchen and garden refuse from the cottage to the landfill site.

- Recycles waste into a valuable gardening product, which can assist in growing your own food.

- Further reduces the carbon footprint, and more GHG emissions, when the addition of the compost increases the productivity of your garden; putting homegrown, organic food on the table!

Finally, think about how composting connects to your cottage greening vision. This reflective exercise alone can take learning in many different directions. What do we now know about composting? What do we need to learn next?

Whatever the project, you can contribute to a healthier environment.

Tips to learn more about greening your space:

- Read labels for toxicity and for the safety of children and pets. Just because a product is "natural" does not mean it is safe for children and pets. Borax, for example, is a mined mineral which is an irritant to skin and eyes, and toxic if ingested. Keep it away from young children and food preparation areas.

- Track the reduction of your carbon footprint when purchasing locally, bulk buying, or growing your own food. Did you know that buying locally grown foods makes a significant difference to the reduction of GHGs?

- Volunteer at your recycling depot to learn about what you can recycle in your locale. Recyclables generally include aluminum cans, tin foil, plastics supporting the recycling symbol, glass, non-glossy paper, corrugated cardboard, cereal boxes, wine bottles, and cork stoppers.

- Surf the Internet to keep abreast with research and what is currently trending and happening in your area, and beyond.

- Attend workshops and forums offered in your community to learn about future projects such as: planting native trees and drought tolerant landscaping, growing your own food, retrofitting for energy efficiency, or, building a new sustainable cottage.

- Learn by exploring and implementing, or putting into action, greening projects at your cottage.

Becoming environmentally savvy, whether learning in nature's classroom, at community workshops and forums, volunteering at the recycling depot, or through daily acts, will improve your greening lifestyle at the cottage. Through ongoing learning, everyone will gain a growing knowledge and a deepening understanding of environmental sustainability.

# 4
# Making a Commitment:
# A Cottage Greening
# Action Plan

*Taken together, our efforts are like drops of dew that slowly accumulate in the soul of the world, hastening the day when the entire Earth, with all its peoples and creatures, will enjoy harmony and fulfilment.*

— Guy Dauncey

Making a commitment is fundamental to realizing your greening vision, and ultimately to the shared responsibility of working towards a sustainable environmental lifestyle at the cottage. A greening action plan puts your commitment into place; it is essentially a contract, or a blueprint, to living your vision and to achieving your greening goals.

# 1. Steps to Creating a Cottage Greening Action Plan

To this point, a process has unfolded to facilitate the creation of your Cottage Greening Action Plan which will be enduring, yet open to improvements along the way.

Figure 9: Cottage Greening Process

To create a Cottage Greening Action Plan:

- Set a greening goal, setting out with the end in mind: What do we expect to accomplish as a result of our greening commitment? (We covered this in Chapter 1.)

- Craft a greening vision to put your goal into context: How will this look, sound, and feel at our cottage? (Also covered in Chapter 1.)

- Take stock of, or assess, current greening attributes and lifestyle habits at the cottage. What eco-friendly and energy efficient attributes and greening practices are in place now? What do you need to change? (Covered in Chapter 2.)

- Learn alongside everyone at the cottage, and teach others in your community, and beyond, about living in harmony with nature, and, greening and environmental sustainability. What do you need to know to work toward an environmentally sustainable lifestyle? (Discussed in Chapter 3.)

- Make a commitment! Develop your Cottage Greening Action Plan. What conscious, consistent actions are needed to work toward an environmentally sustainable lifestyle? Once in writing, so to speak, your planned actions will be relative to key greening strategies which focus attention on why you are doing what you are doing.

## 1.1 Your Cottage Greening Action Plan

Through your Cottage Greening Action Plan you will be consciously implementing key greening strategies to guide your sustainable lifestyle practices: nature conservation, renewable resources, energy efficiency, eco-friendly materials, and reducing GHGs.

An action plan sample exercise follows as Exercise 1; you can fill it out or print off copies from the download kit to use. Choose a format, or adapt a format, that will make sense to you, and one which will guide your actions and ensure your commitment will move forward. Keep it simple.

Exercise 1 shows a simple action plan which is based upon setting out with the end in mind, and prioritizing projects and actions over ten years. Unless you are building a new cottage, it can be practical for budgeting purposes that a greening action plan have a ten-year timeline, or longer (due to constraints such as costs)!

In addition to your goal, your vision, and greening strategies to target, this plan includes: list of projects or actions; determining resources required for each project or action; the projected date for the project or action; and monitoring and assessing the project or action. You may consider these ways to monitor progress:

- Take before-and-after photos.

- Use a journal or log for observations and updates.

- Keep a spreadsheet of data over time such as the volume of recyclables, energy utility bills, amount of rainwater collected, and the cost of renovations and retrofits.

- Log in to your electricity or energy account to track and monitor your electrical/energy consumption.

- Blog your observations and reflections with fellow cottagers or others who are on a similar greening journey.

- Develop your own website or shared cloud folder, to keep all members of your cottage family, or fellow cottagers, up to date with the progress, challenges, new learning, and adjustments happening.

Monitoring the progress of a project or renovation may be as simple as using Checklist 2 (a blank copy is available on the download kit).

Your monitoring and record keeping will provide valuable information which will assist in:

- Keeping your greening commitment.

- Making adjustments to your Cottage Greening Action Plan.

# Exercise 1
## Cottage Greening Action Plan

| GOAL | an environmentally sustainable lifestyle! | | | | |
|---|---|---|---|---|---|
| VISION | Living a "green" environmentally friendly ethos is envisioned as we connect with nature, deepen our understandings, nurture our spirits, and refurbish our little island cottage in its big forest. | | | | |
| TIMELINE | 10 years | | | | |
| Greening Strategies (Targets) | • Conservation of nature<br>• Renewable resources<br>• Energy efficiency<br>• Eco-friendly materials<br>• Reduce GHGs<br>• Sustainable lifestyle (practices) | | | | |
| Project/Actions | Resources<br>• Research/gather information<br>• Consultant<br>• DIY/Contractor<br>• Cost/Estimate<br>• Materials<br>• Others: | Monitoring | Year/Date | Assessment/Progress:<br>• Targets met<br>• Evidence<br>• Quality<br>• Complete/Incomplete<br>• Lifestyle changes<br>• Other: | Notes/Reflections<br>• Lifestyle changes<br>• Review plan and budget<br>• Adjust plan<br>• Other: |

| | | | | |
|---|---|---|---|---|
| Upgrade to dual flush 4.6 l toilet | Cost: $200<br>Plumber: $225 | 05/2008 | | Conserving water. |
| Removal of stumps and dangerous trees | Arborist $200<br>Tree service $6,000 | 07/2009 | Completed Dec. 2010 | Safety; prevention of ant and termite infestation.<br>Yielded 2 cords± of firewood. (value $550) |
| Repair to wood/garden shed; installation of metal roof | Contractor:<br>Materials: $6,016<br>Labor: $6,300<br>Bid:<br>• Sheath 2 x 8 rafter system;<br>• Install: metal roof; gutters, down spouts; re-claimed window; 6x6 electrical entrance post; cedar batons, door & window trim;<br>• Build: fascia, barge board, soffit system;<br>• Clean up and dispose of old/waste materials. | 09/2010 | O/S Finishing trim above entrance.<br>Next steps:<br>• Upgrade electrical panel (200 A to 400 A);<br>• Build ramp entrance<br>• Insulate & line interior of shed. | Use of renewable & sustainable materials, purchased locally. |

- Budgeting for greening investments; large expenditures which are cost-effective in the long term.

- Managing information and dates regarding cottage projects and installations.

- Keeping track of tradespersons.

- Tracking the progress and cost of a project.

- Noting specific energy efficient and eco-friendly products and materials.

- Reflecting on any shift in habits or lifestyle.

Working towards a greening vision is a long-term commitment and it may take a number of years to see your vision fully in place as you journey towards your goal. Monitoring your progress will show the evidence of your actions, one step at a time.

Checklist 2
## Monitoring Progress of a Project

| Project/Action<br>WOOD/GARDEN SHED REPAIR & FINISHING (Roof and Siding) | Date: Fall 2017 | |
|---|---|---|
| Contractor: **Enviro-Joe Contracting**<br>Included in bid: (Included in bid: purchase of materials at contractor rates; removal of old and scrap materials)<br>Estimate: **$12,000.00** | | |
| **Project Status** | **Complete** | **Incomplete** |
| Remove rotted materials: roof, siding, paper | ✔ | |
| Repair/rebuild rafters | ✔ | |
| Install metal roof | ✔ | |
| Install window (reclaimed) | ✔ | |
| Prepare for electrical upgrade | ✔ | |
| Install paper and cedar siding | ✔ | |
| Finish woodshed entrance trim | | ✔ |
| Clean up and removal of refuse, etc. | ✔ | |
| **Total Cost (materials + labor)** | | **$ 12,316.00** |

# 2. Sharing Your Commitment

It stands to reason that you will be wanting to share your greening commitment and learning with neighbors, friends, and family. A great way to do this is to make a cottage-warming green gift for someone moving into your cottage community. The following green gifts can be so much fun to knit by the fire on a rainy day or, interesting to arrange after puttering in the garden.

## 2.1 Green gifting

When you are thinking about that special gift for a fellow cottager, or for someone on your holiday list, think about a green gift. Green gifting is a mindful way to keep your commitment towards your sustainable lifestyle, and help someone else get into the greening movement, too!

Green gifts could be a:

- Native tree, shrub, or perennial.

- Rain barrel.

- Kitchen compost container.

- Recycled glassware or a piece of locally crafted pottery, such as wine glasses, a pitcher, or a bowl.

- Membership to join a local food or nature group which promotes sustainability.

- Cotton shopping bag, or one of another sustainable fabric.

- Homemade jam or pickles from your kitchen.

- Environmental books and guides on cottage greening, and beyond.

- Hemp or cotton hand-knit dishcloths.

- Bird house or bat house.

Be creative, and keep in mind your commitment and the greening strategies. Green gifting is an environmentally conscious action ensuring that less stuff will be inundating our landfill sites, and the conservation of nature and natural resources will not be in jeopardy.

Not only will you observe your neighbor's joy in receiving a green, handmade gift; you will have the opportunity to share your learning and commitment to greening your cottage. It is likely to be catching!

## Project Idea: Hemp or Cotton Dishcloth

Reduce waste by giving a homemade, reusable, biodegradable gift. With this you will be celebrating an occasion such as a neighbor's moving into a new cottage; and, sharing with others your greening commitment!

**What you will need:**

- 2-5 or 6 mm. knitting needles
- 1.75 oz./ 50 g ball of 4-ply hemp blend or cotton yarn (fibers are sustainable and can be laundered at a high temperature to kill bacteria)

**What you will need to do:**

- Cast on 4 stitches
- Knit 2 rows
- Rows 3 through 45* (increasing): k 2; yo; knit to end of row
- Rows 46 1 (decreasing): k 1; k 2 tog; yo; k 2 together; knit to end of row
- Continue decreasing until 4 stitches remain on needle
- Knit last 2 rows
- Cast off
- Finish ends by weaving into body of dishcloth. See Figure 9

(Knitting can take some time to perfect; if you're a beginner, there are some wonderful how-to videos on YouTube.)

**Figure 9: Knitted dishcloth**

---

* The number of rows can be increased or decreased, depending upon the finished size that you desire. This mid-row is the diagonal measurement of the finished dishcloth.

## Project Idea: Mini Herb Garden

Share a part of your organic garden. A mini herb garden makes good reuse of plastic food jars ready to be plant pots, a discarded wicker basket, or a scrap of wood which may be sitting about your cottage and end up in a landfill site. This is a cottage-warming gift idea which will add a culinary touch of greenery to a deck or kitchen, and may become the starter for your neighbor's own herb or kitchen garden.

**What you will need:**

- Plastic jars/pots such as empty peanut butter or mayonnaise containers.

- Small stones or gravel.

- Mixture of soil and compost: four parts potting soil and one part compost (from your compost bin).

- Seedlings and/or cuttings such as basil, chives, parsley, oregano, thyme. (Note that parsley and chives are best started from seed.)

- Wicker basket, or a salvaged piece of wood siding.

- If wall-mounting the mini herb garden: two metal bands for each pot, and two wood screws for each metal band.

**What you will need to do:**

- Drill holes into the base of each plastic pot for drainage.

- Add stones or gravel to lower quarter of pots.

- Fill remainder of pots with soil-compost mix.

- Gently pack soil mixture to approximately 2 cm. /½ inch from top of pots.

- Water until the water begins to drain from the bottom of the pots.

- Let sit overnight for soil to become moist but not saturated.

- Seed herbs or transplant seedlings and cuttings into pots, one herb per pot.

- Grow for one or three weeks in a bright sheltered spot (indoors or outdoors).

- Mist regularly to avoid overwatering.

- Allow at least four weeks if planting from seed and thin to two to three seedlings per pot.

- Present the mini herb garden in a wicker basket; or mount the jars on a piece of attractive salvaged wood with metal bands and wood screws. If there is a handy person at the cottage, building a simple wooden shelf (or salvaging one) could be another way of presenting your green, cottage-warming gift.

- **Note:** Your choices of reusable materials and skills at organic gardening will be in celebration of your commitment to your greening lifestyle as well as a welcoming gift to a new neighbor. Through sharing your practice, you will bring pleasure and inspiration to others. And, you will be reducing your carbon footprint by reducing and reusing materials and growing your own food (even if on a small scale)! Be sure to take note of what herbs flourish best in a small container for future mini herb gardens.

Your Cottage Greening Action Plan is your contract, or blueprint, to living your vision and achieving your greening goal. From now on, you will be implementing and monitoring the conscious sustainable actions outlined in your action plan.

Cottage maintenance, and large substantive projects or renovations are some of the common actions explored in the next chapter.

# 5
# Putting Your Cottage Greening Action Plan into Action

*A sustainable community, and a group of dedicated, passionate souls committed to building it. A solution to the scourge of the twenty-first century, a future worth fighting for, the world we need.*

— Chris Turner

The groundwork has been laid for committing to your cottage greening vision and ultimate goal. Through narratives, or stories, and practical ideas rather than a theoretical discourse, greening had been explored alongside real-life practices and ongoing learning. With a practical knowledge base and examples, the tools for constructing a Cottage Greening Action Plan have been discussed.

Now, you have your Cottage Greening Action Plan in writing. It is important to realize that your Cottage Greening Action Plan is not the end, but rather, it is the beginning of an enduring commitment. You have the action plan or blueprint to greening your cottage. So, now what?

# 1. Our Action Plan in Action

It has been ten years since we purchased our island cottage in the big forest. Our vision was crafted shortly afterwards; and we still see it as the beacon towards a sustainable cottage lifestyle. We found that the cottage inspection report received prior to purchasing, and our later exercise in taking stock, made the creation of our Cottage Greening Action Plan a straightforward process, for the most part. Apart from some immediate minor attention to leaking taps in the pump house, and some inadvertent wind damage in our forest, our greening journey set out in accordance to our action plan.

For the past nine years we have had a Cottage Greening Action Plan. Our commitment to the installation of eco-friendly materials, fixtures, and renovations has been happening. Our first greening project was the installation of a 4.6 liter dual flush toilet to replace an 8 liter single flush tank. Though our well-water supply was more than sufficient, water conservation was something we wanted to act upon right from the start. We could not assume that our water supply would be sustainable with the radical shifts in climate over the past years. Furthermore, water conservation was a greening commitment which everyone at the cottage — children and adults — could make, and, to which we could all commit.

At the time of purchase, the inspection report drew our attention to the need for the installation of gutters on the cottage, and the replacement of the rotting siding and roofs of the garden and water system sheds. This became a substantive greening action, indeed. There was research to do and materials to learn about and consider. A local contractor was hired to install metal gutters to the cottage during our second year of possession. This renovation and upgrade has extended the life of the original cedar shake roof as well as stopped the water erosion around the concrete footings upon which the cottage stands.

Both sheds received repairs, cedar siding, and the rotting roofs were replaced with metal roofing. Metal roofing lasts a lifetime and there is virtually no maintenance required. In addition, metal roofs have an excellent rainwater collection efficiency factor. Metal will also reflect the heat of the summer sun, maintaining cooler interior temperatures. The original cedar shake cottage roof will soon need replacement. The replacement roof will be of the same metal installed on the sheds — ideal for future rainwater collection. We believe that metal roofing is a "greening" investment. It is costly at the moment, yet will be cost saving in the long term.

A compact, energy-efficient front-loading washer and dryer were appliances that we added as well. We also installed a reclaimed aluminum umbrella clothesline/dryer to the outer rail and floor board of our deck. It is removable should we not want it on display, but it is generally on display because it is worth bragging about. This practical DIY project has had a definite impact on our hydro bills, too. As a bonus, we love the fresh clean scent of the air-dried laundry and the sun's bleaching effect on our white socks and tea towels!

We have learned so much about waste management through our excellent local recycling depot. Over the years there have been many changes as to what is accepted as a recyclable material. Plastics and food wrappers have been a challenge at the cottage. Our purchasing habits have changed too, with a conscious effort to reduce the plastics in our shopping cart.

Today, our cottage is 23 years old, and renovations, upgrades, and maintenance projects are ongoing, as is our learning. Budgeting has been greatly facilitated by having our Cottage Greening Action Plan. Our learning has brought us to an understanding that energy efficient retrofits and sustainable materials are a long-term investment. Though the replacement of our cottage's cedar shake roof, to be replaced by a metal one will be a costly project, the metal roof will require next to zero maintenance, and serve for efficient rainwater collection. The annual return on this greening investment will be greater than the interest on our savings investments!

As it is highly unlikely that repairing our 23-year-old appliances and systems is an option, additional soon-to-be substantive greening actions will include the replacement of our major appliances, our hot water tank, and our septic system. We are constantly researching products and items which are energy efficient and materials which are of renewable resources.

Our forest, too, requires ongoing management. It works continuously at detoxifying the air we breathe, provides the cottage with a secondary sustainable energy source, and, offers an abundance of habitat and food for our forest wildlife neighbors. We walk and play about the deer paths, read in the hammock suspended between two giant firs, and just marvel at this amazing gift of nature.

Expert consultation has been sought. Local professionals have been contracted to remove a fir tree which was growing into the roof edge of our garden shed. Now, there are three dead firs which are potential hazards to our cottage. They too will be coming down and will fill our woodshed for the winter. It is worrisome to notice the stress which the

Figure 11: Our Action Plan in Action

trees are experiencing. There has recently been a noticeable effect of a drought upon the cedars. Is this another observable consequence of climate change? We believe that it is paramount to seek professional consultation to conserve our forest.

# 2. Your Cottage Greening Action Plan in Action

Your Cottage Greening Plan is grounded in the pre-actions — your greening practices and consequential learning — which have been happening since you got started with greening at the cottage. Maintenance, improvements, and practical projects have been ongoing. Consequently, new knowledge has been acquired and new understandings have emerged through exploration and practice. Habits may have been adjusted and changed as well. For example, composting may have been a practical project during the pre-plan phase. Now, composting may be an ongoing conscious practice to eliminate the kitchen and garden waste from your trash can.

Making your own eco-friendly cleaning products, reducing recyclables, practicing chemical-free pest control, or water and energy conservation projects may also be in progress at your cottage.

Daily acts of kindness toward nature, ongoing maintenance, and planned upgrades are evidence of your cottage greening journey. With your action plan in action, large, costly projects such as the replacement or purchase of major appliances, or, a septic system upgrade will be forthcoming in as planned a manner as possible.

And, to reduce GHGs, or your carbon footprint, you may find that you are practicing some of the following ways to reduce your carbon footprint at the cottage:

- Plan one car trip to accomplish all your errands.

- Cut back on car trips. Walk to the beach, bike to the market, jog to the mail box, and, kayak or canoe to the neighbor's.

- Buy locally.

- Purchase quality hand garden tools rather than gas-engine driven trimmers and mowers to reduce the use of gas emissions.

- Transform a traditional lawn into a low-maintenance native landscape which does not require a gas-motor driven mower (and watering!).

- Nurture or plant native trees which will remove harmful $CO^2$ from the air. Do you know that $CO^2$ is the predominant GHG produced by human activity, and the greatest contributor to global warming?

The next sections will deal with some specifics.

## 2.1 Substantive greening actions

Substantive greening actions are eco-friendly, usually costly, and planned to meet your greening goal. These actions may target one greening strategy, but generally, a combination of the following greening strategies are targeted:

- Conserving nature.

- Energy efficiency.

- Renewable resources.

- Eco-friendly material.

- Reducing GHGs/carbon footprint.

- Sustainable lifestyle practices.

As substantive greening actions can be costly, this is where "green investing" becomes an important consideration. Take time to calculate the financial costs over the long term: the initial installation costs, on-going maintenance costs, and the energy saving costs. Green investing not only has beneficial payoffs for the environment, but it has proven over time to be cost-effective in terms of monies spent and saved. Green investing will save energy costs, as well as further destructive costs to the environment.

Substantive greening actions need to be carefully researched, and may require consultation with an expert to make the right decisions as you move forward with your Cottage Greening Action Plan. Some examples of substantive greening actions which follow may be a DIY project, or, a contracted project to a local professional or expert:

## 2.1a Renovations, upgrades, and maintenance

Renovations and upgrades often require a significant financial outlay and thorough research on your part. Practically speaking, energy efficient and eco-friendly renovations, upgrades, and maintenance can be costly in the short-term yet cost effective in the long-term. For example, installing a high-efficiency catalytic wood stove will cost more than a less efficient stove, yet with this investment less fuel will be consumed, more heat will be produced, and far fewer GHGs will be emitted into the air.

Did you know that many levels of government, and some energy companies, are offering green incentive or initiative grants and energy tax credits to assist with the initial financial expenditure of substantive greening projects? If you are upgrading or renovating to a renewable energy source, or purchasing an eco-friendly product or appliance, check to see if a grant or tax rebate application is available from your supplier or government ministry. Over time, you will find that your green investment is cost-effective as well as environmentally friendly.

It is always best to seek advice from regional authorities and local experts about sound energy efficient investments, greening strategies, and local zoning requirements. Contractors can be another source of help with these issues. Most building suppliers and home improvement retailers have a wealth of information on what eco-friendly products are available to today's consumer.

Consultation to decide whether a renovation or upgrade will be a DIY project, or one which will be contracted, preferably to a local tradesperson, is important when large substantive projects are in the planning. This decision is usually based upon your level of expertise, the amount of time you have available to work on the project, the cost of the materials, and the affordability of hiring a contractor as compared to a DIY project. When considering the sum of these costs, hiring a contractor may be your best choice because of his or her level of expertise and access to purchasing discounts.

Whether a DIY or contracted project, it must be emphasized, before any renovation or upgrade takes place you will need to know the zoning or building codes in your locale. Whether you are in an incorporated or unincorporated region, your local government representative or a government agency can provide you with necessary zoning information and let you know whether a building permit is required. Most contractors are also sources of this information. Renovations, upgrades, and maintenance can be costly, and you will want to be sure that your green investments are thoroughly researched, carefully planned, and of quality construction and craftsmanship.

When renovating:

- Repair, reclaim, or salvage any current structure, object, or appliance if it is repairable and eco-friendly in nature.

- Replace carpet with natural surface flooring such as reclaimed wood, wood, stone, or clay tile to eliminate off-gassing, for low maintenance, and for sustainable qualities.

- Replace weathered shingles with a metal roof. Metal roofs are low maintenance, fireproof, and far outlive the shingles and shakes of traditional roofing. Metal roofing is ideal for rainwater collection, too!

- Shop for reclaimed and salvaged materials and fixtures, and even cottage furnishings.

- Consider a deck as an additional living space for: eating and entertaining, crafts, yoga, family games, relaxing with a good book, or pitching a pup-tent for kids' sleepovers.

- Maximize natural lighting with large windows and skylights. Dual or triple glaze units increase the insulation factor from summer's heat and winter's cold. Your energy bill will be lower, too.

- Install screens on windows, and a ceiling fan, for passive cooling and ventilation.

- Shop locally.

- Take leftover materials and products in good repair to your local "Re-store" facility.

- Arrange to remove old appliances and hazardous materials such as old drywall, manufactured wood products, or insulation to your local hazardous waste depot. Did you know that if you hire a contractor, removal of old/scrap materials, products, or appliances can usually be included in the estimate?

## 2.1b Eco-friendly heating alternatives

Conventional heating systems generate a lot of harmful GHGs which pollute our air with toxic chemicals. In fact, heating your cottage may be the major contributor to your carbon footprint. Most conventional heating systems continue to be dependent upon electrical energy and fossil fuels. Though electrical hydro energy is eco-friendly, the continuing high production of coal-sourced electricity in many parts of the country is not eco-friendly.

With the growing understanding of environmental sustainability, there is a movement away from fossil fuel sources to sustainable sources. Eco-friendly heating is becoming more available and affordable with improved technologies and the incentives of many levels of governments to move from fossil fuel sources to environmentally sustainable sources. Cottagers are beginning to look for eco-friendly and government supported heating alternatives such as:

- Geothermal heating.

- Active solar heating.

- High efficiency wood heating.

## Geothermal heating

Geothermal heating is a costly specialized installation (usually at the time of construction), and, it is a natural, energy efficient, and highly cost effective system after installation. The source of the heat comes from the earth's constant underground temperature of approximately 12.8°C or 55°F. Though geothermal heating is not simple in terms of technology and engineering, simply described, a heat pump circulates a liquid through an underground piping system where it is warmed by the earth. The warmed liquid is circulated from the ground into the cottage's ducting system, releasing the heat, and returning underground to re-heat. (Geothermal cooling is also part of this process.) Extensive information on geothermal heating is easily accessed through government energy websites, geothermal distributors, and some plumbing and heating businesses.

## Active solar heating

Solar energy is also a natural means to heating your cottage. However, a reliable supply of sunshine and sophisticated installation fittings are factors to explore when considering investing in this eco-friendly heating system (or energy source). Like other sustainable resources, improved technologies, as well as demand, have made active solar heating a financially viable renovation, upgrade, or first-time installation. Solar energy is captured through solar panels usually mounted on the roof. The number and size of the panels will vary with the exposure and slope of the roof, and the amount of energy required to heat the cottage. Simply speaking, within the panels, a heat-transfer fluid is warmed and transferred to a storage chamber. As needed, the heat can be circulated throughout the cottage by a variety of means such as radiators, radiant floor heating, hot water baseboards, or a forced-air system. You can easily access detailed descriptions of all aspects of solar heating (and solar energy), including the pros and cons, through government energy websites and plumbing and heating businesses.

Because the solar panels are mounted on the roof of the cottage, it will likely be necessary to have an engineer's inspection to determine if and what structural upgrading to the roof will be necessary before the installation. Should you be building a new cottage, it is wise to ensure that the roof construction will take the load of solar panels, even if you are not planning to install solar heating/energy until a future date.

## High efficiency wood heating

There is nothing more comforting on a chilly evening at the cottage than a burning log on the fire. However, wood heating is a controversial topic. You must be aware if wood is not burned properly, harmful gases, particularly $CO_2$, will be emitted into the atmosphere. Thus, the retrofit of a certified high efficiency insert in a conventional fireplace, or the installation of a clean-burning, energy-efficient stove must conform to the emission standards of your locale.

A pellet stove is another wood heating appliance that doesn't include a burning log on the fire. A pellet stove is more efficient, cleaner burning, and cheaper to purchase than most certified high efficiency wood burning stoves. The pellets are manufactured primarily from sawdust, a renewable, salvaged, and inexpensive natural material. Pellets also have the benefit of taking up little space for storage, and you will not need to worry about whose turn it is to chop today's wood supply. A wide variety of retail outlets such as hardware stores, building centers, and heating outlets sell pellet stoves as well as the pellet fuel.

Whether you choose an energy efficient wood burning or pellet stove, each appliance must be regularly maintained to ensure continued safety and efficiency.

If you are considering upgrading your current wood stove or your fireplace to a high efficiency wood heating appliance, thoroughly research the pros and cons of wood heating at your cottage. Local experts, as well as Environment and Climate Change Canada and APA US Environmental Protection Agency, have up-to-date research and guidelines which must be followed. Did you know the following facts about wood as an energy resource?

- Wood is a carbon neutral energy resource. That is, trees "breathe in" carbon as they grow, and burning wood releases $CO_2$. (Even dead trees release $CO_2$.) Therefore, the intake and output of $CO_2$ neutralizes the $CO_2$ factor.

- Wood is a renewable resource when it is harvested from a sustainable, managed forest or wood lot.

When using wood heating:

- Check with an expert that your stove or fireplace is an efficient, clean-burning appliance.

- Keep the chimney cleaned as recommended by the appliance or chimney manufacturer.

- Burn only well-seasoned wood, sourced from a sustainable managed wood lot, or from your own mindfully managed property.

- Never allow the fire to smolder. A hot, clean burn will burn off most of the gases, and greatly reduce the amount of smoke emitted.

- Have your wood heating appliance and chimney inspected regularly. Did you know that this is a requirement of most insurance companies?

- Add a self-powered fan to your stove's decor and to increase the circulation of heat throughout the cottage.

## 2.1c Replacement or purchase of major appliances

When the need arises to purchase or to replace major appliances, perhaps a new hot water tank, energy efficiency and reducing the carbon footprint are equally important environmental strategies.

Certainly, there are many manufacturers and retailers offering a wide range of Energy Star appliances: stoves, refrigerators, freezers, dishwashers, clothes washers, and dryers. Check though, as to the amount of water that the dishwasher or clothes washer uses. Some manufacturers claim that their dishwashers and clothes washers consume lower quantities of water. Many building centers sell, or can special order, off-grid appliances for cottagers choosing a self-sufficient cottage lifestyle. Making energy efficient purchases is easier today than it ever has been. What may be difficult is determining what you really need as compared to what you want.

How to reduce the carbon footprint is also important to strategize when making these major purchases. Many cottages are a distance from retailers, and local retailers should be your first choice when making major purchases. When local purchasing is not a choice, keeping deliveries and removals to and from the cottage at a minimum needs to be part of the purchasing plan. If the refrigerator breaks down, for example, would it be environmentally wise to replace the refrigerator and another aging appliance at the same time? There may be a financial saving, too, for buying two appliances rather than one!

## 2.1d Replacement or purchase of a hot water tank/heater

When purchasing a hot water tank or heater, the greening strategies are similar to what they are for purchasing major appliances. The carbon footprint, however, may be considerably less, depending upon the type of tank one chooses. Local hardware stores and heating and plumbing businesses sell a variety of Energy Star hot water tanks. In addition to the conventional hot water tanks, tankless hot water heating has become a common energy efficient means to heating water electrically or with gas. You need to know, however, that when the power goes out, you are in for a cold shower.

Tankless hot water heating is much more energy efficient than the traditional tank method as it heats water on demand and eliminates the ongoing loss of heat held in a large tank and the cottage pipes. It also requires less maintenance, and does not require the draining upkeep of a traditional tank. Did you know that a conventional tank should be drained regularly to flush out collected sediment which builds up over time and decreases heating efficiency and the life span of the tank?

When draining and refilling your conventional hot water tank:

- Turn off the electrical power or gas to the tank.

- Turn off the water supply to the tank.

- Connect a garden hose to the drain pipe at the bottom of the tank.

- Place the hose into the sewer drain, or to the outside of the cottage.

- Open the drain valve at the drain pipe.

- Wait approximately one hour for the tank to drain.

- To refill, close drain valve at the bottom of the tank, and open the water supply tap to the tank.

- Do not turn on the power until the tank is filled.

- You will know the tank is full when hot water comes out of the water faucet.

## 2.1e Septic system installation or replacement

A septic system does not last forever. It is also one of the costliest installation or replacement decisions made at the cottage. In addition to its large financial outlay, municipalities have very specific environmental guidelines regarding septic systems which must be followed. For these reasons, a certified installer needs to be consulted and contracted for this substantive greening action. This does not mean, however, that you do not need to research the pros and cons of various systems, and be well informed as to the local environmental guidelines. In this case, you will have a good understanding of a healthy septic system, and of ensuring that there is no pollution to local water supplies.

## 2.1f Eco-friendly toilet and shower installation or replacement

Until recently, water conservation was a greening strategy which was generally ignored in our bathrooms. Conventional toilet tanks had a capacity of 8–10 liters, or larger, and though showering was generally considered to consume less water than bathing, shower heads often had full-flow settings. You may still have one of these "water-wasters" in your bathroom. If this is the case, or if you are building a new cottage, you will notice that water conserving toilet tanks and shower heads are now the norm. Toilet tanks range from approximately 3.8 to 6 liters. Some tanks also have a dual flush feature which can further reduce the amount of water used when flushing. Look for a low-flow shower head or one that has a water-saving setting.

Humus (composting) and electric toilets are alternatives to flush toilets. These are literally waterless toilets. When you are considering either of these toilets, check that you are purchasing an eco-certified toilet. If it is a humus toilet that you are interested in, you will need to check your local government or municipal sanitation regulations. Humus toilets are ideal for an off-grid cottage, however, they are not allowed in all locales. Like most eco-friendly fixtures and appliances, these toilets are available through building centers, humus and electric toilet manufacturers, and some plumbing and heating businesses.

The results of conserving water in your bathroom will show a significant savings on your water bill and help to ensure that everyone has an adequate supply of water.

These are but a few examples of the substantive greening actions which can be considered in your Action Plan. When such projects are planned for, budgeting can be in place and the financial outlay will not be unexpected. Though, as with anything, in the unfortunate occasion when something major unexpectedly breaks down, the cost may be inconvenient!

More cottagers are planning their greening expenditures over time, and have decided that their greening is an investment in the conservation of energy and resources, and in a reduced carbon footprint. In the long term, energy costs, both financial and environmental, are being saved.

# 3. Reflections: Where Are We Now?

Now that you've set goal(s) and a vision, and have created an action plan and started putting things into place, you can now see, hear, and feel the results of some of your sustainable commitments; yet realize that there is still much to learn, and so much more to do.

Reflect on your growing knowledge of sustainability and deepening understanding of your commitment towards attaining a sustainable cottage lifestyle.

It is particularly interesting to listen to the voices of the youngest members of our family as they hone their developing understanding and growing appreciation for greening at our cottage:

*We stayed at other places on the island before we had our cottage. At our cottage I remember when there was no furniture and I was putting together the wooden stool. In the loft I like to watch the winter rain against the skylight. It is so calming. The hammock in the forest is relaxing. Everything is green — recycling, composting, and conserving the forest are important. I want to keep it that way; every little bit counts. I've learned, too, about the virus which the purple sea stars now have. I appreciate the beach, the wildlife, and the forest. This is where I want to go because it is where I feel a relaxed calmness.*

— E. (15 years old)

*I've been at the cottage forever; since I was really little! When I think of our cottage I can see the forest and the tall green trees and the open space. It's beautiful. For me being at the cottage is relaxing and calming; it is a happy place. There is never a dull moment with always something to do. I want to keep it nice. I pick the broom so that it is shrinking and the good plants can live. Picking is better than using herbicides because the poison would kill other plants, the animals, and bugs. I've learned ways to reduce all our trash. We use to have a great big bag; now we just have a few things. The cottage is where I want to go.*

— K. (12 years old)

Hopefully the reflections at your cottage are as lovely.

# 4. One Step at a Time towards a Sustainable Lifestyle

Greening is not a finite process, nor does it stop at the cottage! (Self-Counsel Press has also published books titled *Greening Your Boat, Greening Your Home, Greening Your Office,* and *Greening Your Community*; all important topics.)

Though you can observe and reflect on tangible evidence that greening is happening where you are, many actions will not be observable for several years to come. There is enough reasonable evidence however, that a sustainable cottage lifestyle can make a positive difference to our environment.

Indeed, there is hope. Nature has made remarkable recoveries throughout the world. Many cottagers are surrounded by nature, or at the very least, have ease of access to nature. With the natural affinity between nature and our children, and adult cottagers too, a prime opportunity to foster a deeper respect for and appreciation of this grand environmental schema lies within every cottager's realm. Our greening actions, whether small or grand, are acts of kindness with nature in mind, and of course these actions will have a cumulative impact on the wellness of our environment.

Today, hope lies within our greening commitment; and tomorrow, in the hands of our children, children's children, and beyond. Environmental stewards living in harmony with nature can achieve a sustainable lifestyle. The practices and lifestyle at the cottage must spill over into the same commitment at home, in our communities, and in our global community. Greening your cottage inside and out is the way towards environmental sustainability, one step at a time.

# Sources and Resources

## Books and Articles

Barlow, Zenobia. "Confluence of Streams." *Resurgence Magazine:* Ecoliteracy Dancing Earth. Issue 226, September/October, 2004.

Bouchard, David and Roy Henry Vickers (Illustrator). *The Elders Are Watching.* Tofino, BC: Eagle Dancer Enterprises Ltd., 1990.

Cockburn, Linda. Living the Goodlife: How One Family Changed their World from their Own Backyard: Tried and Tested Strategies for Sustainable Living. Prahan, Victoria, AU: Hardy Grant Books, 2006.

Cooper, Jocelyn. "The Right Mix: Getting the Most out of Your Compost." Cottage: Recreational Living in Western Canada. Vancouver, BC: OP Publishing Ltd., July/August 2008. pp.22-23.

Covey, Stephen R. The 7 Habits of Highly Effective People. Anniversary edition. New York, NY: Simon and Schuster. 2013.

Dauncey, Guy. "An Extraordinary Threshold". EcoNews. Newsletter #90. Victoria, BC: Earth Future, January 2000. http://www.earthfuture.com/econews/back_issues/00-01.asp

Dole, Klein, Hilary & Adrian M. Wenner. Tiny Game Hunting: Environmental Healthy Ways to Trap and Kill the Pests in Your House and Garden. Los Angeles, CA: University of California Press, 2001.

Goldsmith, Sheherazade. A Slice of Organic Life. New York, NY: DK Publishing, 2007.

Gregory, R., L. Failing, M. Harstone, G. Long, T. McDaniels and D. Ohlson. Structured Decision Making: A Practical Guide to Environmental Management Choices. Hoboken, NJ: Wiley-Blackwell. 2012.

A Guide to Residential Wood Heating. Natural Resources Canada. 2002.

Johnson, Bea. Zero Waste Home: The Ultimate Guide to Simplifying Your Life by Reducing Your Waste. New York, NY: Scribner, 2013.

Kellner, Jessica. Housing Reclaimed: Sustainable Homes for Next to Nothing. Gabriola Island, BC: New Society Publishers, 2011.

Mulder, Michelle. Trash Talk: Moving Toward a Zero-waste World. Victoria, BC: Orca Book Publishers, 2015.

Ryker, Lori (Author) and Audrey Hall (Photographer). Off the Grid Homes: Case Studies for Sustainable Living. Layton, Utah: Gibbs Smith Publisher, 2007.

Schimmel, Schim. Dear Children of the Earth. New York, NY : Cooper Square Publishing Llc., 1994.

Turner, Chris. The Geography of Hope: A Tour of the World We Need. Toronto, Canada: Vintage Canada, 2008.

Ward, Jennifer. I love dirt!: 52 Activities to Help You and Your Kids Discover the Wonders of Nature. Boston, MA: Trumpeter Books, 2008.

## Children's Literature

Beletsky, Les. Bird Songs: 250 North American Birds in Song. San Francisco, CA: Chronicle Books, 2006.

Bunting, Eve and Ted Rand (Illustrator). Night Tree. Boston, MA: Houghton Mifflin Harcourt, 1994.

Drummond, Allan. Energy Island: How One Community Harnessed their Wind and Changed their World. New York, NY: Frances Foster Books, 2011.

Drummond, Allan. Green City: How One Community Survived a Tornado and Rebuilt for a Sustainable Future. New York, NY: Frances Foster Books, 2016.

Eiseley, Loren. The Star Thrower. New York, NY: Harvest Books/Times Books, 1978. p. 169.

McFarlane, Sheryl. Jessie's Island. Victoria, BC: Orca Book Publishers, 2005.

Drake, Jane and Ann Love. The Kids Cottage Book. Toronto, Canada: Kids Can Press Ltd., 1993.

Mulder, Michelle. Trash Talk: Moving Towards a Zero-waste World. Victoria, BC: Orca Book Publishers, 2015.

Rothman, Julia with John Niekrasz. Nature Anatomy: The Curious Parts & Pieces of the Natural World. North Adams, MA: Storey Publishing, 2015.

Schimmel, Schim. Dear Children of the Earth. New York, NY: Cooper Square Publishing Llc., 1994.

Susuki, David and Kathy Vanderlinden. Eco-Fun: Great Projects, Experiments, and Games for a Greener Earth. Vancouver, BC: Greystone Books, 2001.

# Websites

## Visioning, Mind Mapping, and Mission Statements

How to Write a Mission Statement

www.wikihow.com/Write-a-Mission-Statement

Mind Mapping App

https://itunes.apple.com/us/app/inspiration-maps/id510031612?mt=8

# Environmental Sites

Burn Wise/US EPA

https://www.epa.gov/burnwise

Canada Mortgage and Housing Corporation on Insulating Your House:

https://www.cmhc-schl.gc.ca/en/co/grho/grho_010.cfm

David Suzuki Foundation

www.davidsuzuki.org/publications/resources/2011/green-cleaning-recipes/

Eco Kids: Earth Day Canada

https://ecokids.ca/

EnergyStar

www.energystar.gov

Energy Quest Room

www.energyquest.ca.gov/projects/index.html

LightRecycle

www.lightrecycle.ca

Rainwater Harvesting

http://rainwaterharvesting.tamu.edu/calculators/

Self-Counsel Press Green Series

www.self-counsel.com/reference/green.html

Teaching and Learning for a Sustainable Future

www.unesco.org/education/tlsf/

Use Water Wisely

https://youtu.be/pr3-l68c-GE

# Download Kit

Please enter the URL you see in the box below in a web browser on your computer to access and use the download kit.

> **www.self-counsel.com/updates/greencottage/17kit.htm**

The following files are included in the download kit:

- Cottage Greening Action Plan template
- Progress Monitoring Checklist
- Resources for further research and reading
- Closing the Cottage for Winter Checklist
- — And more!

**service@self-counsel.com**